ESSENTIALS OF
SMART PARENTING:
LEARNING THE FINE ART OF
MANAGING YOUR CHILDREN

ESSENTIALS OF SMART PARENTING: LEARNING THE FINE ART OF MANAGING YOUR CHILDREN

DR. CARL G. ARINOLDO

AND

LINDA D. ARINOLDO, M.S.

BOOK ILLUSTRATIONS BY LAUREN A. PERL

Kroshka

New York

For permission to use material from this book please contact us:
Telephone 631-231-7269; Fax 631-231-8175
Web Site: http://www.novapublishers.com

NOTICE TO THE READER

The Publisher has taken reasonable care in the preparation of this book, but makes no expressed or implied warranty of any kind and assumes no responsibility for any errors or omissions. No liability is assumed for incidental or consequential damages in connection with or arising out of information contained in this book. The Publisher shall not be liable for any special, consequential, or exemplary damages resulting, in whole or in part, from the readers' use of, or reliance upon, this material.

Independent verification should be sought for any data, advice or recommendations contained in this book. In addition, no responsibility is assumed by the publisher for any injury and/or damage to persons or property arising from any methods, products, instructions, ideas or otherwise contained in this publication.

This publication is designed to provide accurate and authoritative information with regard to the subject matter cover herein. It is sold with the clear understanding that the Publisher is not engaged in rendering legal or any other professional services. If legal, medical or any other expert assistance is required, the services of a competent person should be sought. FROM A DECLARATION OF PARTICIPANTS JOINTLY ADOPTED BY A COMMITTEE OF THE AMERICAN BAR ASSOCIATION AND A COMMITTEE OF PUBLISHERS.

Library of Congress Cataloging-in-Publication Data
Arinoldo, Carl Guy, 1948-
  Essentials of smart parenting : learning the fine art of managing your children / Carl G. Arinoldo and Linda D. Arinoldo.
    p. cm.
  Includes index.
  ISBN 10: 1-60021-420-7   ISBN 13: 978-1-60021-420-2
  1. Parenting. 2. Child rearing. I. Arinoldo, Linda D. II. Title.
HQ755.8.A725 2006
649'.1--dc22
                    2006026676
      Published by Nova Science Publishers, Inc. ✢*New York*

INTRODUCTION

Parent   education...Parent   training...Parental   instruction...Parental
edification...

Parental enlightenment...or, just plain, old parenting. Whatever you
choose to call it, it all boils down to just one thing---albeit one very important
thing---but, nonetheless, one thing. And, what is that one thing, you might
ask? Well, if you've picked up this wonderful, well-written, informative book-
--and, obviously, you have---and, if we are all on the same wavelength---
which, hopefully, we are---then, that one thing, obviously, is parenting (as if
you didn't already know!). One small word for one very complex and
profound concept.

As we like to point out to all parents, being a parent is the most important
job you will ever have. It is a job that the consequences of which will be felt
by someone (your child), for his or her entire lifetime! Yet, despite these facts,
very few people receive any formal instruction on how to at least come close
to being a smart and effective parent.

And, in most, if not all, cases, some instruction is not only needed, it is a
necessity! Just take a minute or two to think about it. We are all human
beings. And, since human beings are not perfect, then, the conclusion has to
be that none of us is perfect. In addition, since we are not perfect, it stands to
reason that nothing we do will actually turn out perfect (in the strictest
definition of the word). Therefore, wouldn't you agree that some insights,
some guidance, some hints toward being a smart and effective parent couldn't
hurt? Shouldn't hurt? Wouldn't hurt? We hope that you would agree with us
on this issue.

If you are still "sitting on the fence", so to speak, all we ask is that you open your mind and be objective enough to at least consider the fact that there just may be some information on alternative child-rearing practices available that could make being a parent somewhat easier, more enjoyable, less stressful, and, last, but certainly, not least, much more satisfying.

Now, before you get all bent out of shape and, heaven forbid, throw down this book (ouch!!), please hear us out. We are not trying to change the world---although that really wouldn't be such a bad idea. No. We are not THAT ambitious! What we are attempting to do is to merely point out some parenting techniques, or strategies, if you will, along with some related topics, that, in our years and years of experience, we have found to be beneficial for many parents, parents who have been willing to face the fact that they may not have been parenting in a smart and effective manner. And, as such, they were experiencing child-rearing problems, some minor, but also, some not so minor.

In addition to not trying to change the world, we are also not trying to "give you" a perfect family. Remember, just as no one person is perfect, no one family is perfect either. All families, regardless of their make-up, have their own ups and downs, some of which are unique, while others, are not. It is just a fact of life that all types of families will experience some highs as well as some lows. Families will have some serious disagreements and some not-so-serious disagreements. It is also a fact that all parents will, at some point in time, become quite exasperated---no matter how good their children may be.

As we have said, these are the facts. So, acknowledge them! Live with them! Try to adjust to them! But, and it's a big but----DO NOT let them discourage you!

Remember, no one is perfect!

However, following from the aforementioned facts, please realize that, while perfection is definitely not in the cards, so to speak, perhaps improvement is. And, it is this idea of improvement that gives rise to the volume that you are currently reading.

Like we have previously said (or wrote?), we cannot change the world nor can we make your family perfect. But, what we can do is offer some "words of wisdom", or guidelines, if you will, that, when all is said and done, may help to improve and/or strengthen your skills as a parent.

At this point, we feel that a word of caution is warranted. And that word (or words) is: DO NOT BE DEFENSIVE! Let down you guard. No one is calling you a bad parent. No one is telling you that you should have been the last couple on earth to have had children! No one is saying that your children are the worst "kids from hell" that have ever walked the face of this earth! No one is telling you that.......

OK!! OK!! Enough already! We think you get the picture. At least we HOPE that you get the picture.

In short, just put your defenses away, open up your mind, invest some time, and, in the end, you may be quite pleasantly surprised.

Also, please keep in mind that the ideas expressed in this book can be generalized across many different types of child-rearing situations.

Chapter 1

WELCOME.....WELCOME.....WELCOME

Yes. Welcome!...Welcome!...Welcome! Welcome to a wonderful world chock full of quiet, peaceful meals! Welcome to a glorious world where you can easily get your child up for school on time---EVERYDAY! Welcome to a beautiful world where you never experience disagreeable children at bedtime---or anytime! Welcome to a fantastic world in which you have consistently pleasant, compliant children! Welcome to a world of no demands...no misbehavior...no tantrums...no talking back...no stomping of feet! Welcome to the wide, wonderful, fascinating, and delectable world of parenting!!!

Sounds good, doesn't it? Of course it does! However, we think we know what all of you readers are probably thinking right now: "Yeah. Right". If you even so much as picked up this book, purely out of curiosity, mind you, you are probably thinking: "Yeah. Right". We shutter to think that you may also be saying: "What planet did these two just land from?"

Or, "I bet THEY don't have any children". Or, better yet: "These two should live in MY house for just one day, or even for just one HOUR, and then let's see what they have to say!"

These types of thoughts from parents are actually quite understandable. In fact, when you sit in our chairs (as psychologists working with parents, not as authors writing a book), thoughts or responses of this nature are actually to be expected.

But. Really folks. When you do have a quiet moment, albeit rare, to devote to thinking about the GOOD qualities in your children, you will more than likely amaze yourselves at just how many good qualities your children actually have. Please note. We used the word "moment" purely in a semantic sense. We are sure that you will probably need much more time than a moment to assess your children's good qualities and talents.

But. But...but...but...but...BUT! We are not here to talk about good qualities. If we were going to discuss only good behaviors, or qualities, this would be a very, very boring, not to mention, unnecessary, book (yawn). And, for some, a very, very, very brief book.

No. Our objective here is to talk to you (or write to you, whichever you prefer), about matters AFFECTING your children's behaviors. Or, to put it more specifically, YOUR role in your children's misbehaviors. That's right! Your role in those unwanted, undesirable, obnoxious, infuriating, hair-pulling, wall-climbing misbehaviors. You know, the kinds of things that make you wonder, sometimes aloud, what the attraction was in being a parent in the first place!

However, believe it or not, these regularly occurring misbehaviors that most parents frequently complain about, are the kinds of things that many average children exhibit from time to time. They are the kinds of things that parents usually blame for their graying hair, hoarse voice, and/or, spreading middle.

Incidently, if you are concerned about your "spreading middle", you can read our book, "*How To Control Your Eating*". (How's that for some shameless self-promotion!!)

Anyway, these are the types of behaviors that would make life a lot easier and much more enjoyable, for both parent and child, if the behaviors would become more manageable.

So, what are these behaviors, you ask? What are these behaviors that leave you shaking your head in disbelief---not to mention, defeat? What are these behaviors that make you wonder why you tried soooo hard to conceive the little darlings? What are these behaviors that have you and your spouse pointing at each other saying: "He must get it from YOUR side of the family"; or, "I bet YOU were just like that when YOU were a kid; or, "DO SOMETHING!!!"

OK. Stop laughing. You do say these things, don't you? Of course you do.

Most people with children will, on occasion, make these statements, or, at least, something very similar. And, what gives rise to statements such as these, you ask? Well, to be succinct, it's part frustration and part exasperation. In most cases, it just goes with the territory of being a parent with a child or children who exhibit behaviors that, for whatever reason, you, as the parent, just do not understand and find difficult to deal with.

It's all part of the package, the package that you have filled, covered, wrapped, and delivered---to yourself! But, rest assured, It doesn't have to be this way. It doesn't have to stay this way. The situation can change. Your understanding of and ability to handle problem situations involving your children, can, with some serious dedication and application on your part, improve dramatically!

Now, before going any further, permit us to answer the abovementioned question (there was a question back there someplace, wasn't there?). Oh, yes. The question was:

"What are those behaviors that we will be discussing in this book"? Well, for the bulk of this book, we will actually be discussing, as we have alluded to above, characteristics of YOUR BEHAVIOR! Why your behavior? Because, your behavior has a direct and profound effect on the behavior that you will see exhibited by your child or children.

Thus, as we will point out in this book, if you change your own behavior from ineffective to smart, where parenting is concerned, then, and only then, will your child's or children's behavior also change! You must be the one to make the first change if you expect your child or children to likewise change.

Now, toward the end of this book (see, "Ask the Psychologists", Chapter 15) we will address some specific difficulties that many parents face from time to time. And, as you will notice, some of the difficulties spoken about are probably the result of ineffective, or, "not-so-smart" parenting, while others are more a function of something beyond the child's---and the parent's---control, yet, things that must be dealt with.

These difficulties would include the following:

1. Child's academic functioning declining for no apparent reason.
2. Child throwing temper tantrums.
3. Child not making friends and/or being socially immature.
4. Child losing interest in reading.
5. Adolescent's relationship with parents changing.
6. Sibling arguments.
7. Children wanting too many material things.
8. Child's language not understandable.
9. Child is overactive.
10. Adolescent's behavior and attitude negatively changing.
11. Etc.

Do these types of difficulties sound familiar? They should. Some, most, or all of these annoying difficulties, loosely put, occur in more homes, with more children, than you would ever believe. Your home is not the only home where these things happen. At times, it may seem like it is, but, believe us, it is not. There are millions of homes in this world in which you will find tired, worn-out, frustrated, exasperated parents who are facing the same types of problems with their children as you are probably facing with yours. So, our dear friends---you are not alone!

At this point, however, we would like to digress for a moment to a related issue regarding misbehavior. When discussing what constitutes misbehavior, there is one thing that definitely should be kept in mind. That one thing to consider is that, what constitutes misbehavior in one household may be perfectly acceptable in another.

For example, one set of parents may not be disturbed in the slightest if their child did not clean up his or her room---at least on a semi-regular basis. On the other hand, another set of parents may find this behavior to be totally disgusting and clearly intolerable. Also, one set of parents may not be too concerned about their children's bedtime, while others may have a significant problem with this issue. In actuality, it's all really quite relative, given the family and it's particular lifestyle.

However, a word of caution seems to be in order here. While some parents are more tolerant and accepting of certain questionable behaviors exhibited by their children, parents need to be very careful as to where they draw that line of acceptability and tolerance. It's been our experience over the years that many parents make the mistake of unwittingly drawing that boundary line a little too far to one side, the inappropriate side, and hence, smack into the territory of unwanted misbehavior. Consequently, the result is that these parents set themselves up for the very problems that they then have to try to get rid of later on! It makes absolutely no sense, whatsoever!

Still, other sets of parents may draw that boundary line too far to the other side, also inappropriate, thereby pushing THEMSELVES into the overly rigid and strict category. When this is the case, you can stake a bet that, as in the above scenario, significant problems will eventually ensue.

So, what is the "correct", or appropriate place to be, you ask? Well, in realistic terms, that "correct", or appropriate place will be different for different families, depending, first, on the parents and their ability to smartly and effectively parent, and second, on the types of children they have. Remember, the average parents with average children do not want to sway too far to either side of whatever is average. If the parents are too far in either direction, they will be asking for problems that they really do not need. Life is tough enough. Why make it tougher by parenting at one extreme or the other. Again, it just doesn't make sense!

Now that we have sufficiently digressed (as we do from time to time) let us return to the issue of not being alone in your parenting endeavors. Just knowing that you are not alone may be of some consolation. Also, the prospect of knowing how to smartly manage your children's behaviors would also be somewhat comforting. These aspects, taken together, should serve to increase your motivation toward changing whatever it is that needs changing, in order to succeed in your attempts at successfully managing your children's behavior.

But, make no mistake about it. As we have said and/or implied thus far, making the necessary changes is not an easy thing to do. It is time-consuming. It takes perseverance, dedication, and, "nerves of steel". But, tell the truth--- don't you think it will be worth it to sacrifice your time and energy today in order to help make your life easier tomorrow?

We definitely think that it is! And, IT CAN BE DONE! Look at it as an investment for the future---both your's and your children's.

Think about it. You take the time and make the effort to secure a better financial future for yourself, your spouse, and, your children. However, that type of investment usually involves earning enough money, carefully spending what is earned, saving for college, etc.

Well, to put it bluntly, the investment in your children's behavior is just as, if not more important than anything monetary. Who cares if you have the money to send your children off to the best colleges? What's really important is that you send them off TO LIFE with a strong sense of what's right and what's wrong; with good moral values; and, with a healthy respect for other human beings!

And, where does this all start, you may ask? Well, it starts with you at home by giving your children a sound foundation through teaching them to know the difference between appropriate and inappropriate behavior, AND by teaching them to put the appropriate learned behaviors into action. Like we have stated before, parenting is the most important job you will ever have. You are your children's first teachers. Make the most of the opportunity!

Chapter 2

THE THREE P'S
PREPARE...PREPLAN...PREVENT

OK. At this point, you've probably already decided that your children misbehave. What a revelation! Also, you have probably come to the conclusion that it is finally time for a change. And, if you're reading this book, that's probably a good conclusion to come to!

Now, as the title of this chapter notes, it is time to PREPARE...Now, it is time to PREPLAN...Now, it is time to, hopefully, PREVENT. Yes, it is now time to prepare, preplan, and, hopefully, prevent those misbehaviors that are driving you right up the wall. Note: We say "hopefully" because, like most everything else in life, there are never really any guarantees. We just try our best.

So, as we continue, please remember those three "P's": Prepare...Preplan...Prevent.

And, just in case you haven't guessed as yet, the first two of the three "P's" involve YOUR behavior. The third, of course, is trying to prevent your children's misbehavior---or, at least as much of the misbehavior as you can!

With this book in hand, keep in mind that you are already preparing and preplanning. Yes...That's right! Just by picking up this book and reading it, you are preparing and preplanning, to a certain degree, for those tasks that lie ahead. By heeding what you will be reading in this book, you should be well on your way to changing your own behavior with the hope of preventing many of those unwanted behaviors exhibited by your children.

Please keep in mind, however, that NOTHING, absolutely NOTHING (short of a muzzle and/or harness) can be guaranteed to work well in controlling every acting-out behavior that a child will exhibit. Note, again: We are not advocating muzzles and harnesses! But, with systematic, thoughtful preparing (reading this book) and planning, not to mention CONSISTENT follow-through, your chances for prevention and/or improvement will probably be very good, if not, excellent.

Now, if you have been reading closely, which we hope you have been, you will notice that we have mentioned that all-important word, "CONSISTENT". And, vowing to be consistent is part of your preplanning. As you continue reading through the following pages, you will see that we will mention the word "CONSISTENT" over and over again. You may get sick of that word, but, that's OK. You need to learn it and act on it!

Why so much emphasis on one particular word (CONSISTENT)? Why is this concept of consistency so important? Why should you be aware of this term and fully understand its meaning and implications? Well, very simply. It's THAT important!

But, unfortunately, it really isn't all that simple. In fact, being consistent may very well be the single, most important, yet, most difficult concept in the world of parenting to master. But, once mastered, it can produce very, very effective results. Of course, other techniques are also important, but always with consistency as the main ingredient.

Throughout our many years of working with children and their parents/families, we have observed that, time and time again, the parents who achieve the most success in controlling their children's behavior, are the same parents who understand what it means to be consistent, and, who acted consistently whenever they have to discipline their children.

We have also found that it is not good enough to be "a little consistent", or to be consistent "some of the time", or, even to be consistent "most of the time". No. These variations on "consistency" are really not what consistency is all about. Consistent means just that---CONSISTENT!!

So, please bear in mind that, in order for you to have a stab at achieving success in your quest to be in control of your children's behavior, you must be consistent ALL OF THE TIME! Yes. You read that sentence correctly...ALL OF THE TIME!! There is just no substitute for total consistency. There is no other degree of consistency that will work for you or for any other parent reading this book. Nothing short of 100% consistency is required.

Now, we realize that this all sounds so ominous and scary. How could it not? How could it not make you feel more than a little apprehensive when you are told that you must do something all of the time---100% of the time! When you are told that, in this area of consistency, you cannot falter; that you cannot waver; that you cannot make mistakes in being consistent, it does seem quite ominous.

And yes, we would agree, it is a gigantic task to be consistent. But, it is not impossible. And, you will probably find that the more consistent you are, the more consistent you will become. More than likely, you will also discover that, with practice and serious application, you will probably find it easier and easier to be consistent.

One note to remember. If you do happen to "slip up" once in a while in your attempts at being consistent, it won't be the end of the world. Just resolve to pick yourself up and try to be fully consistent in the future.

OK...We can almost hear you saying to yourself: "Sure, consistent for someone else, but definitely, not for me!" And, you may continue to say: "Well...Maybe I can be a little consistent, but, only if someone waves a magic wand!" If this is the case, all we can say is don't sell yourself short. Don't despair. Don't defeat yourself before you even begin. You must be positive and think positively.

You CAN learn how to be consistent. You really can! With awareness as to what your own behavior consists of, and, with perseverance, you, too, can become one of those successful, consistent parents.

But, please do not misunderstand us or make the entire endeavor much more difficult than it has to be. Keep in mind that, in the long run, most clear-thinking parents are generally successful to one degree or another. Our goal is to try to help you make your journey a little bit easier.

Chapter 3

C. A. P.
CONSISTENCY...AWARENESS...
PERSEVERANCE

While you are digesting, and, hopefully, preparing to commit to memory, the concept of consistency, there are two other key points that must be addressed: Awareness and perseverance.

According to most dictionaries, awareness can be loosely defined as being "knowledgeable or conscious about something, anything". And, the word perseverance can be summarized as "pursuing one's goal despite any obstacles that may arise".

So, how do awareness and perseverance apply to you as a parent? Well, quite simply, these ideas apply to you because, as we have previously noted, in order to change your children's behavior, you have to change your own behavior first! Or, to put it another way, you have to change whatever it is in your own behavior that needs to be changed in order to accomplish your goal of smarter and more effective parenting. Consequently, it is of utmost importance that you be fully aware and conscious of your own behavior at all times, especially when your interactions with your children are in question.

You must know (be aware of) *exactly* what you did or said, in response to a misbehavior, so that, after the fact, you can go back and review the situation to determine what, if anything, went wrong. Maybe nothing went terribly wrong. That would be great! But, if something did go wrong, you'll want to know what that something was. Once this is determined, you must then persevere in your efforts to correct, on a consistent basis, what needs to be corrected.

Now, to help you out a bit with your interactional review, we have found that, by asking yourself the following questions, the job of reviewing may be somewhat easier.

Ask yourself:

When my child did---or said---"X", "Y", or, "Z" (you, of course, would fill in the "X", "Y", or, "Z"):

1. What was my IMMEDIATE interpretation of the situation?
2. What was the very first thing that I did or said after my child did or said whatever it was that he or she did or said?
3. What did my child do or say after I did or said something?
4. What was my tone of voice?
5. What was my child's tone of voice?
6. At this point, did the situation get resolved amicably?
7. If not, did the situation seriously escalate?
8. Why do I think the situation escalated?

Now, before you become unnecessarily frustrated with the above task, allow us to more fully explain the aforementioned steps. So, follow along while we attempt to ease your frustrations and concerns.

1

Let us refresh your memory by reiterating the first question listed above: "What was my immediate interpretation of the situation?" When reviewing your interaction with your child, remember that perceptions can, at times, be deceiving. Specifically, your child's past behaviors may "color" how you are interpreting the situation at hand. In other words, your interactional history with your child may be unduly influencing your perceptions of the current situation rather than perceiving the current situation as it truly happened.

If this is occurring, you must put a stop to this line of thinking. Instead, you must examine EACH situation only in terms of exactly what happened DURING THE SITUATION IN QUESTION. You have to keep everything in the present so your perceptions have an excellent chance of being realistic and, above all, accurate.

Now, please do not misunderstand us. We are not saying to forget about and/or ignore your child's past misbehaviors. What we are saying is to leave the past in the past ---at least while you are wrestling with a current episode of misbehavior. The time for recalling your child's past misbehaviors is when you are determining the frequency of a misbehavior and deciding on the consequences to be implemented. Other than that, keep your interpretation in the present.

2

The second question noted, again to refresh your memory, was: "What was the very first thing I did or said after my child did or said whatever it was that he or she did or said?" Got that? We hope so. In our experience, we have found that a parent's initial, or first reaction (either behavioral or verbal), serves as an enormous precipitating factor in whether or not the incident will continue as well as the intensity at which it will continue.

Keep in mind that it is extremely easy to impulsively blurt out something that will only serve to escalate the situation with your child. It is also quite easy to impulsively make some type of a gesture or movement that will also escalate a situation. Remember, body language can speak volumes--- and, sometimes, more than the words themselves!

This is why it is so important---soooo very important---to carefully and objectively examine *exactly* what you did or said during those first few crucial moments with your child. And, if what you either did, or said, or both, DID escalate the situation, then you must fully examine your own behavior (verbal and nonverbal) to begin to understand how YOU may be bringing about the very situations that you are seeking to eliminate!

3

Moving right along, allow us to get to the third important question: "What did my child do or say after I did or said something?" If your child responded negatively and you can link your child's negative reactions directly to how YOU inappropriately initially reacted (see #2), this would give you a strong clue concerning the specific behavior in yourself that needs some changing. If you can identify this part of the puzzle, then, in the future, you may be able to end a situation before it escalates into unpleasantness.   So, the moral of the story? Nip the situation in the bud by learning to control YOUR first reaction in the first place!

4 AND 5

Continuing with our explanation, our fourth question to be answered was: "What was my tone of voice?" And, since this question deals with the same idea as the fifth, i.e., tone of voice, we will take the liberty of dealing with both questions together. So, let us reiterate the fifth question. Thank you, we will. That fifth question was: "What was my child's tone of voice?"

Tone of voice is very important when dealing with anyone. But, since we are discussing children, we will keep the discussion on children. While trying to determine the dynamics of a recent altercation with your child, you must try to remember how you sounded. Was your tone of voice firm, yet friendly or was your tone cold and distant? You also need to determine if your tone was condescending, demeaning, or insulting?

It is very important to correctly identify what tone of voice you exhibited, and, if your tone needs monitoring and changing for future interactions, then, CHANGE IT! Being aware of how you sound to your child, and making sure that you are not sounding mean, nasty, or uncaring, can go a long way in avoiding unnecessary problems.

By the same token, try to remember how your child sounded. Somehow, we would guess that you will probably be better at recalling how your child sounded as opposed to how you sounded. Anyway, you must determine if your child's tone was disrespectful and nasty. Or, was your child's tone OK? If your child's tone of voice was questionable, at best, then you must determine if you changed your tone, for the worse, in response to your child's less-than-acceptable tone.

If this is actually what had occurred, then make it your business NOT to again fall into the trap of reacting to your child's negative tone by becoming more negative yourself. It is not an easy thing to do, but, it can be done. With awareness (there's that word again), you can learn how to keep your own tone of voice in the acceptable range regardless of how your child is sounding at any given moment.

6

As we continue, our sixth question: "Did the situation get resolved amicably?"is really quite easy to answer. Obviously, the answer is either "Yes", or, "No". If the situation did get resolved in an amicable manner--- great! Then, whatever you initially said or did worked. So, common sense would dictate that, if this type of situation arises again in the future, the first action for you to take would be what you just did. It's that simple!

However, if the situation did not get resolved to your satisfaction, then, this is not great. In fact, it stinks! (How's THAT for a real professional term!) And, if no resolution is forthcoming at this point, then, you need to proceed with the seventh question.

So, assuming the worst possible scenario, let us continue.

7

That seventh question: "Did the situation escalate?" is also an easy "yes" or "no"answer. Obviously, if you get to this question in your analysis, the situation probably did escalate. And, as such, the eighth question will then come into play.

8

So you don't have to turn back the pages, we will repeat the eighth question for you: "Why do I think the situation escalated?" When pondering this question, it is time for some serious brainstorming. What? You don't know what brainstorming is? OK, we'll tell you!

Just in case you don't know, you can think of brainstorming as coming up with as many reasons as possible as to why whatever happened, happened. No matter how silly or insignificant a possible reason may appear, put it into the mix. You never know. In the final analysis, that silly, insignificant brainstormed idea may be the answer you are looking for.

Now, as you spend some quality time brainstorming, write down all the reasons you have come up with. Then, select two or three of what appear to be the most plausible explanations for the aforementioned escalation. Then, if and when the same, or a similar situation arises, you now know what NOT TO DO if you want the situation to be readily resolved.

And then, if you find yourself and your child in the same or similar place, try a new tactic, assess the situation afterwards, and, if your new behavior worked in keeping the situation under control, then you've got something! You have a new strategy to add to your growing list of smart parenting techniques. However, if what you THOUGHT was the reason for the escalation, wasn't the reason, then more brainstorming would be in order.

Remember, you may have to go through these questions a number of times with each misbehavior until you strike gold. But, once you hit upon the true reasons why your negative interactions with your child escalate into all-out war, you will then be well on your way to preventing such occurrences in the future.

Keep in mind, if you are truly aware of your environment---and your actions within that environment---then, and only then, will you be able to answer the aforementioned questions realistically and accurately.

At this point, a word (or two) of caution appears to be warranted. Namely, DO NOT EMBELLISH on your analysis and make very certain that you stay anchored in reality throughout the analysis. The very last thing that you would want in your assessment, is to unrealistically embellish, create assumptions, and then, act on those assumptions!

Now, when attempting to assess a recent altercation with your child, you may not, at first, be able to remember every detail of your "run-in" with your son or daughter. As such, you may not be able to answer all of the questions posed. No one can remember every single aspect of every single situation right off the bat.

However, with practice (and we're sure that, if you are reading this book, you WILL have ample opportunity for practice), you will be able to develop the skill of being completely aware of what transpired between you and your child, and thus, be able to recall all the details when you want to recall them.

OK...Now that you have some idea of the questions to ask yourself when trying to dissect an unfortunate interaction with your child, there is a closely related issue that we would like to touch upon. And, what is that issue, you ask? Well, even if you didn't ask, you just know that we are going to tell you anyway! Don't you? Of course you do.

So, directly stated, the area of concern that we are speaking about has to do with your physical presence while the interaction was in full swing. In more concrete terms, this issue involves aspects of your bodily, or physical position, in relation to your child's space. (One of us can't stand that word--- "space"---in relation to people. But, it seemed like the only word that would easily fit. Incidently, can you guess which one of us can't stand the aforementioned word? We may tell you later, but, we're not promising anything!). As we go through this, remember that these items should also be incorporated into your assessment of an interaction with your child that, somehow, went wrong.

First of all, when talking with your child, were you sitting or standing? With this question, obviously the height of your child must be taken into consideration. For example, if your child is somewhat shorter than you, perhaps you should sit so you can be on a more even plane physically. Likewise, if your child is about your height or taller, standing would probably be the better alternative.

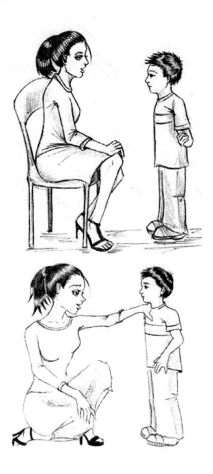

Get the picture? In other words, position yourself in relation to your child's height. Keep in mind that, if your child is young (and probably short), you do not want to be "towering over" the child during an interaction. This can be quite intimidating, not to mention, scary, for the young child, and, it can easily throw the child on the defensive, which, in turn, can cause a situation to escalate.

Another aspect to consider is how physically close you are to your child, whether sitting or standing, whichever is more appropriate (see above). In general, it is fairly good practice to be relatively close to your child during a "discussion" about your child's misbehavior---not on top of your child, mind you, just relatively close. You know your child best, so, use your judgment on this.

This!

Not This!

If you are across the room, you will, more than likely, have to raise your voice to be heard (see "Tone of Voice", above). Once your voice is elevated, and elevated only because of distance, you set the stage for your child's voice to start raising. And then, guess what? An altercation can easily erupt---all solely through a misunderstanding of voice level. So, the moral of this scenario is to stand or sit in a spot from which you can be easily heard without raising your voice.

Continuing on our journey through your physical presence, examine your eye contact. Did you make eye contact with your child or did you avoid that dreaded, for some, eye contact? It is generally good policy, when speaking to anyone, to maintain good eye contact. So, in relation to an interaction with your child---MAKE EYE CONTACT! Not to do so will tend to undermine your own authority. So, if eye contact is not one of your strong points, then you need to practice making eye contact with others.

Finally, you want to be aware of touching your child---LIGHTLY---on the shoulder or arm while speaking to him or her. We stress, LIGHTLY! However, you know your child. If you happen to have a child who does not like to be touched, then, we suggest that you use your common sense and good judgment in this area.

But, for most children, a LIGHT touch during and/or after a verbal interaction carries a lot of positive impact. It is usually seen as a loving gesture, and, it helps to convey, nonverbally, that no matter what the child did, the child did not lose your love.

This is a very important message to get across to ANY child---particularly to the ones who misbehavior. It's like separating the deed from the doer. In other words, the message would go something like this: "You are our son/daughter and we love you very much. This will never change. BUT...That doesn't mean that we have to like and accept your behavior!"

At the risk of repeating ourselves, we would like for you to keep the following in mind. It is generally a good idea to review ANY altercation that you have with your child---whether you were successful in "keeping a lid on things", or not. If you were successful, you can look at the interactions for that situation and study them in order to see exactly what you did or didn't do, or did or didn't say, that made you a success that time out. Then, if desired, that same behavior can be used in the future, should the same or similar situation arise.

In other words, you can add your successful behaviors to your "repertoire of strategies", to be called upon when needed. And, as we have said before, with consistency and practice, the time will probably come when you can call upon the needed strategies quite easily to help you in your "battle of wits" with your children.

Now, all of this sounds great! Doesn't it? Of course it does! And, believe it or not, there actually are times, however few at first, when you will be successful with your children on the very first try. But, for the many times that you are not successful on that all-important first try, our second point---PERSEVERENCE---comes into play. And, like parenting itself, perseverance is no small feat.

As we have previously said, perseverence takes nerves of steel. It also takes a lot of "tongue biting". In addition, perseverance can require some very good acting on your part. Indeed, perseverance can be very difficult to accomplish---difficult, but definitely, not impossible. Keep that in mind!

When you decide on the various techniques that you feel will work well with your child, or children, you <u>must</u> apply them again, and again, and again---if you are going to see any positive results. A parent cannot decide upon some new way of dealing with his or her child, try it only once, try it twice, or, try it only three times, and expect to see satisfactory results. Granted, as we have stated above, on very rare occasions with very rare children, once or twice may work. But, more often than not, it will take many, many repetitions of the same strategy, put into operation by you, as the parent, before you will see positive results.

In short, you must give any new strategy a good trial run before you can decide whether or not the strategy was working in managing the misbehaviors in your household.

When you do find the strategy that works, go with it. However, if a particular strategy is not working to curb some behavior, then you must try other things. Whatever you do, do not give up and let the misbehavior continue unabated.

Remember, each child is different. What works with one child will not necessarily work with another. Even with children in the same family, parents may have to use different techniques with different siblings in order to successfully manage/control their children's behavior. Thus, the point of all this, and the point to be remembered, is to PERSEVERE!

So, to quickly review, whenever you are dealing with your children and their misbehavior, you must:

1. Be <u>C</u>onsistent;
2. Be <u>A</u>ware; and,
3. <u>P</u>ersevere.

Notice how ingeniously we ordered these three concepts into the acronym CAP: Consistent…Aware…Persevere. Just remember CAP!! (Forgive us for borrowing consistency from the previous chapter. We did this to make our acronym work. Besides, it's our book, so, to us, it's OK!!)

Chapter 4

UNITE!!

Hopefully, you have taken to heart the information contained in the previous chapters. If not, the information will always be there for your quick reference whenever you need to refer back for some assistance. So, at this point, let us turn our attention to another concept that can fall under the umbrella of preparing and preplanning. That concept is one of unity.

The idea of unity is very important in the realm of parenting, especially when a child has caregivers in addition to the parents, such as, grandparents and/or day-care providers. Right behind being consistent, being aware, and persevering, is the idea of unity. However, keep in mind that unity, in and of itself, has equal importance with the other three aforementioned ideas of consistency, awareness, and perseverance.

By unity we mean, working together; agreeing on a course of action (prepared and preplanned) for when your child misbehaves; and, uniting as ONE in the execution of said action. We just cannot stress this idea enough. While the concept of unity seems simple in it's meaning, the execution of the concept can be quite different---to say the least.

Keep in mind that it is very, very important for your children to get the distinct message that there is unity between and among ALL the adults--- especially between you, as the parents---who have some type of significant authority over them. Yes...Authority!

Unfortunately, today, in some circles, the idea of "authority over children" (better known to us as discipline), appears to be an old-fashioned, out-of-date concept in child rearing. However, in our professional view, SOMEBODY has to be in authority, or, if you will, in control, when it comes to shaping the behavior of children.

In our humble, albeit professional, opinion, authority/discipline should not be out-of-date. Authority and discipline are of utmost importance in order to try to avoid utter chaos and bedlam in the household. Remember, SOMEONE HAS TO BE THE PARENT---and, that someone IS NOT YOUR CHILD!

Many times we hear parents say that they and their children are the "best of friends"! This idea of being best friends with you children is ridiculous! You can be friendly---yes. But, best friends---NO! Being the "best of friends" is the job of a peer---not the role of a parent. A parent MUST BE A PARENT!! If you want to have a friendship with your children, wait until they are at least out of adolescence. Then, you can be friends all you want. But, until then, BE THE PARENT!!

All children must know that there is someone who is in charge and in control. Someone who has the authority to make the rules, set the limits, and, ultimately, enforce those rules and limits. Contrary to what your children may want you to believe, they actually feel better knowing, at some level deep down inside, that you, the parents, are there making and enforcing the rules in your attempts to teach them right from wrong. When all is said and done, you, as the parents, hope that your children's behavior will, for the most part, stay within the acceptable limits SET BY YOU!

As may be hard for most parents to believe, the aforementioned knowledge in children actually helps them to feel safe, secure, cared about, and, most of all, loved.

This knowledge also helps them to exercise, when the time is right, of course, some age-appropriate, independent behavior, without any unnecessary fear, because, they will know that, if problems develop, you will be there with the "safety net", should they need one.

At this point, let us return to the original topic of this chapter---that of unity. As we have previously stated, it is of the utmost importance that, as parents, you band together in your attempts at disciplining your children. Specifically, your child must, without exception, understand that, if he or she does or says "A", then, "B" will always occur, REGARDLESS of which parent happens to be present at the time of the doing and/or the saying.

For example, if the child throws a temper tantrum, screaming and yelling and carrying-on all over the place (of course, without the possibility of the child getting injured), the point to get across to the child is that mother AND father will handle the tantrum in *EXACTLY THE SAME MANNER*, whenever this kind of behavior occurs.

Thus, your child will not be successful with his or her tantrum with mother but not with father, or, with father but not with mother. In short, the temper tantrums will fail in the presence of EITHER parent as well as in the presence of both parents. By acting in a unified manner, you will quickly defuse the "divide and conquer" routine.

And, as noted above, anyone else who cares for your child, either on a regular or on a semi-regular basis, must also do "B" whenever "A" occurs. It's really the only way to most efficiently and effectively take care of misbehavior. It is essential!

Now, do we hear you asking: "What is "divide and conquer"? Well, whether we do or not, allow us to enlighten you. "Divide and conquer" is simply a child's way of splitting his or her parents down the middle with the same request, suspecting (and, obviously, hoping) that he or she will probably get opposing responses/decisions from each of the parents.

Now, let us warn you that most children, no matter how good they are or appear to be, will, at some point or points in time, try to get away with this "divide and conquer" routine. So, what do we have to say to the parents? BE PREPARED and PREPLAN! Be prepared for this occurrence and plan for it.

If you anticipate it coming at some point (and, we're warning you now), you must be one step ahead of your child, with---guess what---UNITY!

To make this concept as clear as possible, let us spell out how "divide and conquer" works.

Scene: Your son wants to play his video game instead of doing his homework. Obviously, his main objective is to get what he wants, namely, to play the video game. He sees that his mother is in the living room and that his father is busy in another part of the house---close enough but not in the same room. Now that the scene is set, here is the possible dialogue that will probably ensue:

Boy to Mother: "Mom, can I play my video game for a while before I do my homework?

Mother: "Absolutely not!"

Boy: "Aw, common mom. Just for a little while?"

Mother: "I just told you, NO! Now go to your room and get started on your homework. GO!"

Boy: "But why not?"

Mother: "You know why not. Your homework is more important and must get done first. Now, get to it! You can play your video game later!"

Boy: "Oh, come on, please…just a little? I promise I will do my homework right after. Really"! (Smart kid!)

Mother: "Now for the last time, I said NO! Now stop bothering me and go do what you are supposed to be doing!"

At this point, the boy, who is probably noticeably pouting, stomps off to track down his father. So now, Act II can begin:

Boy: "Hey, dad. Watcha doin?" (The pouting has turned into a smile.)
Dad: Mumbles something resembling hi.
Boy: "Is there anything I can help you with?" (Knowing that there isn't. Still a smart kid, don't you think?)
Dad: Grunts something, again.
Boy: "Dad, I'd really, really, really like to play my video game for a while. Can I…can I…please?"
Dad: "What did you say, son?"
Boy: "I said that I wanted to play my video game now, just for a little while."
Dad: "Well, I guess it'll be OK."
Boy: "Gee, thanks dad!

Meanwhile, mother just happened to hear some or most of this verbal interchange between the young lad and his father. With an angry, astonished look on her face, mother yells over to her husband as she enters the room, thus beginning Act III:

Mom: "What do you mean it will be OK? I just told him that he COULDN'T play with his video game. Don't you know that he ALWAYS has homework to do?!"
Dad: "I didn't know that he had homework to do. He didn't tell me!"
Mom: "HE DIDN'T TELL YOU!! OF COURSE HE DIDN'T TELL YOU!!!"
Dad: "No, he didn't" (Father is becoming somewhat sheepish.)
Mom: "It's a weeknight! How could you even THINK that he didn't have any homework tonight? Doesn't he ALWAYS have SOME homework to do? Well, doesn't he?"
Dad: "But…"
Mom: "But, nothing! You never back me up when it comes to YOUR son! You always give in to his every whim! You never…

Now, while this tirade is taking place, their son quietly sneaks off to his room to---you guessed it---play his video game. The message has come through to him loud and clear: He has won another round! He has succeeded in dividing his parents on this issue of whether or not he could play his video game.

In short, he has succeeded in getting the focus of his parents off of himself and onto each other. The whole issue changes right before his eyes and the child gets to do exactly what he initially wanted to do, which was to play his video game. Of course, in these types of scenarios, the child may just want to do nothing at all. The bottom line is that the child just does not want to do what the parent wants him or her to do.

"Divide and conquer" is very easy for children to learn when the parents are not united. Yes, it is very easy to learn, and, for the child, it is very effective. And, unfortunately, once it is learned, it is very difficult to stop.

Does all of this sound familiar? It probably does. The "divide and conquer" routine is a very popular technique used by kids in homes throughout the country---perhaps, throughout the world. Why is it so popular, you ask? Well, from the child's perspective, it is popular BECAUSE IT WORKS! And, it usually works quite well.

And, why does it work so well? It works so well because the parents ARE NOT UNITED IN THEIR EFFORTS!

So, as we have stated above, a unified front is usually the best "weapon" parents can use in order to reduce and/or eliminate this classic routine.

At this point, parents are usually asking the following two questions:

1.   Suppose one of us does not agree with the other, what do we do then?

AND

2. How and when do we settle these disagreements without fueling the "divide and conquer" thing in our kids?

These are two very good, and very important questions that are intertwined with each other, and, your response to one is usually closely related to the other. First of all, whenever an issue arises involving your children and their behavior and you realize that you do not agree with what your spouse is saying, DO NOT---we repeat---DO NOT DISAGREE IN THE PRESENCE OF YOUR CHILDREN! NEVER! NEVER! NEVER!! This will only lead all of you---children and parents alike---directly into the very thing that you are trying to avoid---namely, "divide and conquer".

Instead, when you disagree with whatever your husband or wife is saying to the child, keep your mouth shut! As difficult as it may be to do, do not say anything. Do not make any gestures. Do not roll your eyes. Do not cough (unless, of course, you really have to). Do not snicker. Do not do whatever you may have been doing to indicate your disagreement. In short, remain silent and unresponsive.

If your child turns to you and asks for your input, just redirect the child back to your spouse. You can say something like: "This is between you and your mother", or, "You heard what your father said". If these statements need repeating, then repeat them! But, remember, you must refrain from editorializing or commenting. If you refrain and control your spontaneous desire to "chime in", the child will get the message that you should be sending---UNITY!

Now, if you happen to be fortunate enough to have a very persistent child, which some parents do, then   YOU need to be just as persistent in your stance. You cannot back down and fall into old, more familiar patterns of disagreeing with your spouse in the presence of your child when the issue is your child.

And, you must remember that, if, in a weak moment, you do happen to fall victim to the frustration of being bombarded by your child's whining, by now you should know what will happen---"divide and conquer" will again rear it's ugly head.

So, all of this brings us to the second question, the gist of which was, how and when can you settle those disagreements regarding your children, if you can't disagree in front of them?

Wait! Stop! Hold it! Cease! Halt! We forgot something! Yes, us! We actually forgot something! We forgot to tell you that there are times when it is OK to disagree when the children are present. For instance, when you and your spouse disagree about something that does not relate directly to the children, such as, when to water the lawn, or, where to spend a holiday, or, how to arrange the furniture, etc., it would be fine to discuss these issues with the children present---obviously, in a civilized manner!

When the two of you can discuss a situation or disagreement, weigh the pros and cons of various actions, and then, come to a mutually agreed upon decision, the children witnessing this are, in effect, learning some valuable lessons. They are learning the correct way to disagree with someone; they are learning how to problem-solve; they are learning how to arrive at a meeting of the minds in an appropriate manner, without any bad feelings resulting between the two people involved; and, they are learning that there may be more than one way to resolve a problem.

But, one word of caution appears to be needed here. Whenever the two of you discuss an issue with the children in ear-shot, make sure the issue is appropriate for their ears. In other words, issues such as family finances, insurance, bills, etc., should not be the topic of conversation when the children are present.

Now, lets get back to that second question which we mentioned somewhere in the previous paragraphs. Just to refresh your memory, that second question was: "How and when do we settle disagreements concerning the kids without fueling the 'divide and conquer' thing?

To answer this question, we will state the following. Discuss all of your child-related disagreements when you are SURE that your children cannot hear a word of what you and your husband (or wife, depending on who is reading this) are saying---NOT A WORD!

To say (or write?) this another way, you should wait until your children are asleep (but, speak quietly), outside playing, at school, at a friend's house, etc., before you begin to discuss your disagreements. If the kids cannot hear you disagreeing with each other about something that pertains to them, they will then, more than likely, believe that the two of you are unified in your thinking. And, where there is unity, there is strength!

OK…OK. Just in case you are thinking: "How am I supposed to remember all of this information after reading through all these pages?", we will take this time to summarize the key points/words that you should keep in mind:

-	aWareness	W
-	pErseverance	E
-	aWareness	W
-	cOnsistency	O
-	uNity	N

Awareness: Be fully aware of your own behavior and actions/reactions.

Perseverance: Do not give up in your attempts at using new, more effective behavior.

Awareness: As above. While this aspect is very important, putting it in twice helps our acronym! And, just in case you missed it, our acronym is: WE WON!

Consistency: Be consistent. Apply your new behaviors each and every time your children's misbehavior occurs.

Unity: Unite! Work together in your disciplining efforts. If one parent disagrees with the other, the disagreeing party should keep quiet while the children are within ear-shot. Wait until there are just the two of you to QUIETLY discuss your disagreements.

AND…Do not forget:

PREPARE…
PREPLAN…
PREVENT!

Chapter 5

THE LEARNING-BEHAVIOR CONNECTION

It has been our experience that reasonable, caring parents are usually somewhat knowledgeable about many of the common sense types of things that regularly arise as a child is growing and developing from infancy through to young adulthood. For example, if it's a rainy day, most parents would not send their child out without some type of rain gear, such as an umbrella, a raincoat, or boots. Also, when a child is hungry, the child gets fed. Likewise, when a child needs medical attention, a good, caring parent would see to it that medical attention is given. There are, of course, many more of these types of examples, but, we think you get the idea.

However, to put it bluntly, this common sense thing IS NOT the subject of this part of the book. We are not going to discuss something that parents would know solely by virtue of having good judgment and common sense. And, if you even picked up this wonderful book, it definitely shows that you probably do possess the aforementioned traits to one degree or another. Yet, many parents would generally not see a connection between learning and behavior unless that connection was pointed out to them directly.

And, that is precisely what we intend to do with this chapter---point out the connection,between learning and your child's behavior.

However, please do not misunderstand, or underestimate, the term "learning" as we will be using it. Keep in mind that the term, learning, in our context, does not refer only to the knowledge your child acquires during formal education in a school setting.

Naturally, this IS learning. However, the term, learning, as we will be using it, also encompasses a complexity of issues that may or may not be obvious to many parents. So, please follow along as we explain.

First of all, learning begins where it should begin---at the beginning of your child's contact, or interaction, with his or her environment. As soon as your baby takes that all-important first breath, learning, in the traditional sense, begins. Granted, the learning is in it's most basic, elementary form, but, it is, nevertheless, the start of your child's learning experiences. And, as your child grows and develops through childhood, adolescence, and into adulthood, many more meaningful learning experiences will continue to take place, thereby adding to your child's then-existing and ever-growing knowledge base.

Also, in keeping with our emphasis on learning, we would like to point out that an individual's learning experiences should and will continue throughout his or her lifetime. All one has to do is to look for them!

Now, to continue. As the child interacts with his or her environment, that interaction does not only refer to interactions solely with other people. Your child's interactions with all types of objects are also quite important to his or her cognitive and physical development. Thus, whether the child's environment, at any given point in time, consists of another person or persons, or some type of object or objects, that interaction with person and/or object, can, in and of itself, produce learning.

Following from this, the act of learning something through the aforementioned interactions and experiences, should, in turn, motivate the child and increase his or her desire for additional learning. Then, as more interactions occur, the child continues to learn, and, the motivation to interact remains strong, thus allowing this cycle of learning to continue.

As you can readily see, there is a complex reciprocal relationship between the environment and learning. (And, as we have stated, this interaction generally continues throughout life. But, since we are discussing children, we will stick with children and not venture into the world of adult learning, per se.) To illustrate our point, consider the following scenario.

Your eighteen month old child is walking around the house---supervised, of course! He or she focuses on an object for the first time. Perhaps that object could be a lamp in the den that, up to that time, the child essentially ignored. However, this time the child takes an interest in the lamp, examining it and touching it (lightly, we hope). As your child is examining the lamp, new brain cell connections are being made. These new cell connections will form the basis for your child's new-found knowledge of discovering the lamp!

Clearly, the expression on your child's face tells you that he or she is pleased with what he or she has just experienced. The child has now found something new, something that has previously not been in his or her repertoire of knowledge. Thus, after carefully examining the lamp, and, with a little "instruction" from you regarding what this object is, your child has now learned "a little something" that the child did not previously know.

Obviously, this new-found knowledge pleases the young child. Now, mind you, your child, more than likely, will not be able to tell you in words: "Hey, mom! This is great! Now I know what a lamp is!" But, as we noted above, the facial expression will be all that you will need to understand what has just happened. This small act of learning subsequently motivates the child to explore further. As the child continues to explore, he or she further interacts with the environment, and, consequently, the child continues to learn about that environment and everything in it.

OK. Now that you have a loose---very loose---description of how learning can take place, we can now return to the original intent of this chapter. What was that original intent, you ask? Well, the original intent of this chapter was to point out the specific connection between learning and your child's behavior and/or misbehavior. In the process, we will also note some of the difficulties parents can inadvertently, and easily, get into that can make your parenting efforts somewhat more problematic.

Perhaps, one of the most important things to remember in the learning realm is this: DO NOT PUSH THE CHILD. Again---DO NOT PUSH THE CHILD. That phrase should be committed to memory, and, as quickly as possible! (Just a note---we are not talking about physically pushing the child, folks. Please do not take us literally here, OK?) The second part of this concept is this: DO NOT PUSH THE CHILD BEYOND HIS OR HER PHYSICAL AND/OR COGNITIVE CAPABILITIES. Pushing is bad enough. But, pushing beyond what the child is cognitively and/or physically able to do is even worse.

Just take a moment and think about it. You wouldn't ask a four year old child to put a pail full of garbage out by the curb for pick-up. Nor would you ask a three year old child to take your vacuum cleaner and vacuum a room. These things sound silly, don't they? Well, you can be sure that these actions, along with a host of other things, are not only silly, they are outright ridiculous. And, believe it or not, these types of "requests" can, and do, occur in some homes. OK. Maybe not to the extreme as we have outlined, but, we did need to make a point!

Now, we know what you are probably saying after reading the above words---at least we think we do. (We're not clairvoyant. But, sometimes, it seems as though we come close!). So, to continue, you're probably saying or thinking: "I would NEVER ask my young child to do anything like that. Those things involve physical ability and strength. I would never ask a small child to strain himself or herself with such ridiculous commands. My child could easily get hurt."

Yes, this piece of the child-rearing puzzle may seem obvious to you. But, as we have previously noted, it is not so obvious to some. Think about the young boy who can't hit the broad side of a barn with a baseball. Yet, dad is convinced that he has a future major league player on his hands. Also, consider the child who is absolutely not musically inclined. Yet, the child taps on a table a few times and mom is already picking out her dress for the child's opening at Carnegie Hall!

Think of the child who has great difficulty with schoolwork, not because she "goofs off", but because she simply finds the average work too difficult to comprehend. Yet, the parents will insist that this probable "C" student bring home nothing but those glorious "A's" on her report card.

These are just a few examples of how parents can---wittingly or unwittingly---push a child beyond his or her cognitive and/or physical talents. What parents may not realize, however, is that their actions and desires can be quite detrimental to their child's learning and development. In some children, the aftereffects of inappropriate pushing will be evident in a relatively short period of time, while, in others, it may take a substantial amount of time before the parents will see a behavioral, not to mention, emotional problem arise.

Either way, the situation and the effects on the child, will not be positive. In cases where parents are unsure about what would constitute inappropriate pushing, they should speak with a qualified professional to discuss their specific situation. A licensed psychologist, the child's pediatrician, or, the child's teacher would probably be a good person to contact, or, at least, a good place to start.

As we have alluded to above, there can be some harmful effects on your child that can be traced directly back to this issue of inappropriate pushing.

But, as if you didn't notice, we haven't as yet described what those harmful effects could be. So, if you are with us, we are ready to explore some of those problems. However, please keep in mind that what follows, is not an exhaustive list of difficulties that may arise. These are only SOME of the issues that you may see develop in a child.

To begin with, we will talk about the frustration that can build up in a child who *perceives* himself or herself as being forced, or coerced, into doing something that the child *knows* he or she really cannot do (see Chapter 8 explaining perceptions). In actuality, the feelings of frustraton tend to underlie all of the negatives that follow.

Frustration is definitely not a very good feeling. Try to put this concept into your own terms based on your own experiences. You won't even need to dig back into your childhood for those events. Adult experiences of frustration will suffice.

So, as we have suggested, think about your own history. Have you ever had something---or someone---stand in your way, so to speak, and block you from pursuing or attaining a desired goal, a goal that you felt was very important? Have you ever been given a task to complete for which you have had absolutely no training, yet, you realize that severe consequences will result if you did not adequately complete that task? Have you ever tried to buy tickets to a concert or a baseball game, only to find out that, after waiting on a long line, the person just ahead of you in line bought the last ticket?

As you can probably see, these types of situations, among others, can, and probably would, produce a great deal of frustration in you. So, just as an adult can become frustrated, so, too, can a child experience frustration. And, if you are an average person, what will usually follow feelings of frustration? The simple answer to that is, ANGER!

Whether an adult or child, when frustrated, one usually becomes angry. Of course, the degree of anger will most likely be different for different people, depending on the person's temperament and on how well he or she has learned to deal with frustration. And, as you might have already guessed, frustration-based anger in a child can very easily manifest itself in behavior problems; behavior problems, that, in the average child, could probably have been avoided had the child not been placed in a frustration-producing situation in the first place.

Frustration that results from pushing a child beyond his or her capabilities, can, and usually does, lead to another related problem: The avoidance of learning. In other words, many frustrated children who feel that they cannot perform up to the expectations of their parents, may begin to avoid learning situations. When this occurs, the children tend to adopt a "what's the use" type of mentality where learning is concerned. The child will "reason" that, if he or she can't perform as required because the abilities just aren't present, then, why bother trying at all? Why ask for more rotten feelings? That just doesn't make sense.

This attitude, when present, will lead to an additional problem. It will quickly extinguish the child's motivation to learn. It will easily damage the child's self-concept and self-esteem. And, this type of attitude will also be detrimental to the child's sense of self-confidence.

As you can readily see, these frustration-related problems can be enormous, with far-reaching negative effects, not only for the present, but also, for your child's future. In addition, in terms of behavior, you, the parent, will also experience negative effects because you are the one who will have to deal with the resulting misbehavior! Thus, the moral of the story? DON'T PUSH!!

To continue, the frustration that a child experiences as a result of the aforementioned pushing, is not the only type of frustration that a child can be exposed to that can have dramatic effects on his or her learning and behavior. Another frustration, along with the behavioral consequences, that we have seen throughout the years involves children who have undetected learning problems that, had they been addressed in a timely manner, probably would not have resulted in the development of behavior problems.

When you think about it, it makes perfect sense. If a child cannot learn much, or some, of what he or she is being taught in school, that child will become frustrated, probably angry, and, let's not forget, bored. Thus, this child will, more than likely, use his or her "learning time" misbehaving because he or she cannot use the time to learn.

And, as the learning problem becomes worse, guess what? The resulting misbehavior will also worsen. When this occurs, it is highly likely that the misbehavior will be "carried home" for you, the parent, to handle. As before, all of this can have a major negative impact on future learning, the child's motivation, his self-concept, his self-esteem, and, his self-confidence.

With all of this in mind, it is our professional opinion that, any child suspected of having any type of learning problem, should have a complete evaluation by a certified/licensed psychologist, as soon as possible, to determine if a true problem does, in fact, exist, and, what the nature of that problem might be. Once ascertained, then some type of remediation can be put into place.

Since we have mentioned self-concept, self-esteem, and, self-confidence several times in the above paragraphs, we cannot go any further without saying a few words about these concepts.

All three of these are interrelated and usually have a dramatic impact on a child's developmental, educational, and learning experiences, both at home as well as in the classroom. For the record, and, contrary to popular belief, self-concept and self-esteem are not the same thing. Many people do use the terms interchangeably, but, they do not mean exactly the same thing.

To put it as simply as possible, the self-concept answers the question: "Who am I"?, while the self-esteem answers the question: "How do I feel about who I am"? As you can see, the self-esteem brings feeling and emotion into the picture. Needless to say, fair-minded parents would generally want each of their children to have a positive self-concept and a positive self-esteem. And, if these two entities are positive, then, it would usually follow that the average child would also be self-confident---perhaps not confident in everything, but, much more confident than not.

In addition, a child with a positive self-concept, positive self-esteem, as well as a good healthy dose of self-confidence, can usually develop an "I can handle it" attitude. These children tend to view themselves as being in control of their environments rather than seeing their environments as being in control of them.

This is a huge lesson for them to learn. And, we might also add that, while this type of attitude is quite significant for children, as we have said, it is also quite significant for adults, as well.

Now, in order for a child to have the opportunity to fully develop a positive self-concept and positive self-esteem, and, in keeping with our relationship to learning, any learning problems must be identified as early as possible. And, as previously noted, once a problem is identified, then the appropriate interventions can be put into place in order to remediate whatever that problem might be, and, hopefully, help to restore the child's self-concept and self-esteem. In the long run, the self-confidence should also recover.

Remember, the earlier a child gets the help he or she requires, the greater the probability that the child will attain his or her maximum potential.

However, please note that it is not our mission in this volume to delve into all of the possible learning problems that can affect a child. We will leave that for another book. But, regardless, the important thing that bears repeating is that, whatever the problem may be ---learning and/or behavior--- get it diagnosed and appropriately remediated as soon as possible and as early as it can be done, given the problem area. Once taken care of, the positive effects on the three aforementioned areas (self-concept, self-esteem, and self-confidence) will, more than likely, begin to appear.

And, just in case you have forgotten what was discussed prior to the issue of learning problems, permit us to make another point: Pushing a child beyond his or her physical and/or cognitive capabilities, will, more than likely, lead to serious problems with self-concept, self-esteem, and self-confidence.

OK. Now that we have had our say on these three important areas and before we close this chapter, there is one more issue that we believe needs to be addressed in relation to learning and a child's behavior problems. Over the years, we have found that parents sometimes, again wittingly or unwittingly, may ignore the problems that their children may be experiencing. And, we believe that there are probably as many reasons for this as there are parents who fit into this category. Some of you may know who you are and some of you may not. Whichever it is---*listen up!*

DO NOT IGNORE ANY suspicion of a problem. Do not ignore any problem your child may be having. And, do not ignore any problem that you SUSPECT your child may be having. Don't be defensive; don't point fingers of blame; don't argue about the issue; and, for your child's sake, don't be even slightly concerned about what anyone else might say about your child and his or her difficulty.

Remember. This applies to family, relatives, friends, and/or neighbors---ANYONE! It is absolutely none of their business. Your foremost concern as parents must be your child and seeing to it that he or she is given any and all help that he or she needs when he or she needs it!

So, again...DO NOT IGNORE A PROBLEM. It will not "go away" on it's own. If there is a problem, something needs to be done. And, as the parent, it is up to YOU to start the ball rolling! And, while we're on the subject, if your child's teacher approaches you about a possible problem brewing, listen to what the teacher has to say. The same aforementioned missives (defensiveness, blame, etc.), also apply in this instance.

Now, we know we did imply that the immediately preceding topic of not ignoring a problem was going to close out this chapter. However, as is usually the case with one of us (again, guess which one), something else comes to mind that is considered to be relevant to the topic at hand. And, to be as efficient as possible, where would you put an afterthought? Why, you would put that afterthought at the end of the respective chapter, after the thoughts that preceded the afterthought! Got that? If not, just keep reading and don't bother with the previous sentence.

Now for that last item (we think!). As you may recall, up to this point in the current chapter, we have discussed pushing children; frustrations; and, the interaction of undetected learning problems and behavior, among other things. And, as you also may recall, we talked about the avoidance of learning situations. And this gets us to our last point for this chapter which is related to the avoidance of learning, although it manifests itself in a somewhat more subtle manner. What are we referring to, you ask? Well, we are referring to a reluctance to learn---as opposed to an avoidance type of situation.

With avoidance, the child may act in a more obvious manner in attempting to avoid a learning situation. The child or adolescent may often feign illness in order to stay home from school. He or she may start out for school in the morning but take a detour and never arrive there. This may occur on a daily basis or once or twice per week. Or, the child or adolescent may openly say: "I am not going to school".

Naturally, these are just a few instances of avoidance, but, believe us when we say that children, regardless of age, can be quite inventive when their goal is to avoid learning.

On the other hand, in our view, reluctance is somewhat different. Reluctance tends to be more passive than avoidance, and less "in your face". For instance, a child may "accidently" oversleep and miss the school bus. Or, a child may take an unusually long time to eat breakfast, all the while hoping to miss the bus. Another child may "forget" his or her books in school, books that the child needs for homework or to study for an exam, and so on.

As we have noted throughout this book, our examples are by no means exhaustive. And, as parents can attest, kids can be quite inventive in their attempts to reach their goals, regardless of what those goals may be. Thus, while not so obvious, parents need to keep a watchful eye for these types of behavior patterns. Patterns such as these are usually signals to the parents that some type of problem may be brewing, or, more often than not, is already present. And, just to be clear, we are talking about patterns of behavior---not single instances.

OK. So now we have finished this chapter. However, as is our custom, if something else comes to mind regarding the contents of this chapter, you just know that we will find someplace to put it! But, for now, we do think we are done and ready to move on to the next chapter. Don't forget to move on with us!!

Chapter 6

BEWARE OF THE DREADED WARNING!

There is something special about the issue of giving warnings to children. In fact, in our experience, we have found that parents are so enamored with the idea of issuing warnings, that they just warn…and, warn…and, warn…and, warn. They tend to warn so much that they end up sounding like that proverbial "broken record" (before CDs, folks, records broke). It's a wonder that any disciplining ever got done with all that warning!

Along with all this warning, parents also can usually be heard saying something to the effect of: "If I've told you once, I've told you a THOUSAND times"; or, "How many times do I have to tell you to stop"? Or, how about: "I've warned you for the LAST TIME!" Yeah, like it's really going to be the last time. Don't laugh, this is precisely what your children will be thinking.

Laugh if you will, but, warning ad infinitum is certainly no laughing matter. As a matter of fact, when there are multiple warnings for a child to cease and desist from some misbehavior, you, the parents, are, more than likely, increasing the very behavior that you want your child to stop. In reality, you are working against yourselves! So, stop with all the warnings! ONE warning will suffice. In fact, there should only be ONE warning. After that---ACTION! In other words, after one warning, then some appropriate disciplining strategy should be put into action.

If your household is like many other households then, what is probably happening now in your home goes something like this: Your child does something that you consider to be a misbehavior. You warn. The child doesn't stop. You warn again. Again, the child does not stop. You warn a third time, and, guess what? The child STILL doesn't stop. We could keep going but we think you have the idea. Too much warning really doesn't do a thing. We really shouldn't say that too much warning doesn't do a thing. It does do something---it annoys the h?#* out of everyone, yourself included.

So, listen up! Actually, read up! In order to be effective controlling your children's behavior, you must take stock of how many times you warn them about certain unwanted behaviors. If you come up with an answer that is "more than once", you are warning too much. Once is definitely enough. Any more than that and you are setting yourself up for problems.

You see, one warning should suffice. When you give one warning about the consequences that will ensue if the behavior continues, and then you take appropriate action if the behavior does, in fact, continue, then, your child will get the message loud and clear. And, what is that message, you ask? Well, that message to the child is the following: "If I continue to do whatever it is that I am being told to stop doing, then mom and/or dad will do (whatever the consequence may be). So, If I don't want_____(you fill it in) to happen, then, I better stop doing what I am doing".

Now, prior to this occurring, the parents must agree on what consequences will be put into action (unity, anyone?) if and when certain misbehaviors are exhibited by the children. Once the specific misbehavior and appropriate consequence are agreed upon, then it is time for the parents to have a talk with their child or children.

During this talk, the parents should outline for their child or children which behavior or behaviors will no longer be tolerated. And, for each behavior, the parents need to also outline for their children exactly what the consequence will be. Then, of course, if clarification is needed, then clarification must be done. In addition, the parents should conduct this meeting, if you will, in a friendly, yet firm, manner. Your credibility is at stake!

And, as you prepare for this wonderful conversation, please remember the ideas that we discussed way back in Chapter 3, regarding your physical presence in relation to your child, whenever you are having a serious talk with him or her.

To continue. Following the aforementioned informing meeting, AS SOON AS a behavior in question INITIALLY occurs, that is when the child gets his or her ONE warning to stop. If the behavior does not stop, then, the consequence for that misbehavior that was outlined in the above meeting, must be immediately put into operation. Nothing short of this will work to stop the misbehavior.

At this point, you may be wondering what all the fuss is about with this one warning thing. Well, we'll tell you. If a parent gives a warning several times for a child to stop doing something, once the second warning is out of the parent's mouth, the child begins to get control of the situation. In other words, with repeated warnings, the message that the parent is really sending is this: "I really don't mean what I say. You can keep on doing 'whatever', until YOU feel like stopping".

From the child's point of view, it will come across as: "She really doesn't mean what she says. Mom is always telling me to stop but she never REALLY does anything about it. Oh, sometimes she will punish me. But, I don't think it's going to be THIS time". So, the net result is that the parent is screaming, the child is doing precisely what he or she wants to do, and, nothing productive gets accomplished!

If the child KNOWS that, after the first warning, something will, indeed, occur, then you will, more than likely, see a significant reduction in the behavior in question. It probably will not happen overnight, but, once that message of one warning gets through, the changes can be dramatic.

Needless to say, this "one warning" thing should be added to your growing list of behaviors that the smart parent will need and use.

Chapter 7

THE ART OF DISCIPLINE

OK, folks. Now that you have been made aware of the importance of giving just ONE warning to a child when some type of misbehavior is occurring, not to diminish, of course, everything that had come before "one warning" in this book, we think it is now the appropriate time to discuss a very closely related issue---that of discipline. However, prior to continuing, we would like to point out that it is not our intention with this chapter to cover specific misbehaviors and relate them to specific disciplinary strategies. No, this is not our intent.

Our intent with this chapter is to give you some basic "rules of thumb" that, when consistently adhered to, can make your job of disciplining your children somewhat easier, not to mention, more successful. It is our hope that you will come away from this chapter with some basic disciplining knowledge that you can use time and time again with almost any type of misbehavior that may occur.

And, needless to say, these "rules of thumb" should be incorporated along with all of the other parenting concepts discussed in this book. If this is done, you will have at your fingertips various ideas that, when used correctly, can greatly enhance your parenting effectiveness.

Of course, it should be noted that, as with any "rules", there are going to be exceptions. But, with the average child with average misbehavior, these ideas should be widely beneficial. So, with all of that said, let us begin.

RULE OF THUMB #1

Start Small and Build

As we begin our discussion of the rules of thumb, we would like to point out that this first rule, "start small and build", is, in general, not really given much consideration in many households. In fact, it has been our experience that many parents aren't even aware of this concept. What we have found in our discussions with parents over the years, is that, when a child misbehaves, he or she is usually "hit with" (not physically, folks) both barrels right off the bat. Holding back somewhat---while still disciplining---does not appear to be an option in many instances. But, it should be!

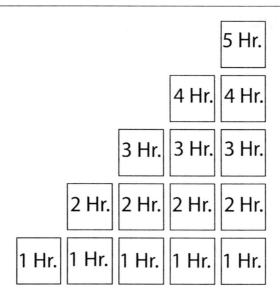

By starting small we mean taking whatever discipline strategy you, as the parent, are going to use, and try to break it down into smaller blocks, so to speak. Of course, this "breading down" would have to be done PRIOR TO the misbehavior actually occurring (preparing and preplanning!), so that, if and when the misbehavior does occur, you will immediately be ready with appropriate discipline. Let us give you an example of how this first rule of thumb would work.

We will assume that you have already decided that there is a misbehavior that you cannot tolerate any longer and for which you have decided on a specific discipline, should that misbehavior occur. And, just as a reminder, since this seems as good a place as any to remind, you should let your child know what that intolerable misbehavior is and what the discipline will be, PRIOR TO instituting any action. Then, as the previous chapter notes, ONE WARNING is the limit!

Now, to continue. Your child misbehaves. You yelling: "You're grounded for one week", would not be starting small. This would be starting BIG! Too Big! And, more often than not, starting big usually works against the PARENTS---not the child. If a child is grounded for a full week, chances are that, by the third day, he or she will not have much of a memory as to why he or she was grounded in the first place---given the child's age, of course. In fact, if this type of grounding is done with relative frequency, your child will probably have a whole host of things ready to occupy himself or herself with during the "grounding" period.

In addition, during the course of that week, something may occur that would necessitate the parent taking the child out of the house, but, with a statement such as: "When we get home, the grounding will continue"! At this point, the parent may be fooled into thinking that the child will understand the continuity of that grounding. But, especially with a young child, the child's perception would probably be: "See...I knew mom wouldn't stick to her guns"!

So, the net result would be an undermining of your authority, not to mention, your word. Do this enough times and see how much longer you'll be taken seriously. And, in many instances, the original misbehavior will probably increase! So, START SMALL! And, how do you start small, you ask? Well, follow along and we'll tell you.

Instead of grounding for one full week, you may want to change that to grounding for the remainder of the current evening. If the misbehavior occurs again, just add a couple of hours to the length of time of the original grounding. If it happens a third time, increase the time accordingly. In other words, start small---rest of the evening---and slowly build up the time--- adding hours---if the misbehavior gets repeated.

Just think how many disciplines you can get out of that original week. Instead of one big block of discipline, which, in the end, probably will not work, you can get a number of smaller blocks of discipline, which will, more than likely, have the effect you are looking for. Several small, appropriate punishments will have a greater positive effect on behavior than one, inappropriately large punishment.

So, you should rethink your discipline/punishment strategy. Remember, you really do not have to "throw the book" at your child each and every time a misbehavior occurs. The only thing you may accomplish is to end up with a child almost immune to discipline.

RULE OF THUMB #2

Do Not Repeatedly Threaten

This rule of thumb ties in directly with the previous chapter on warnings. Hopefully, you will recall that our professional position on warnings is that one warning is the limit, if, of course, you want that warning to carry some weight. Well, this second rule of thumb, if not followed, would, more than likely, lead to the same consequences for you, as the parent, if you continuously threaten without backing up your words with the disciplinary measure being threatened.

And, as you may recall, those consequences include your authority being undermined; your word not counting for much; and, your child perceiving himself or herself as the "victor" in these misbehavior situations. Again, the message comes through loud and clear to your child: "Mom and/or dad really doesn't mean what she and/or he says. If mom and/or dad REALLY MEANT_____(you fill it in with the threat), she and/or he would have done something by now".And, as you may recall, this is exactly the type of message that you, as the parent, DO NOT want to send to your children. So, if you must resort to a threat of disciplinary action, make it only ONE THREAT! Then---ACT! (Appropriately, of course.)

RULE OF THUMB #3

Use The "Misbehaved-with" Item as Part of the Discipline

This rule is really quite straightforward. If the child misbehaves with his or her bike, take THE BIKE away---not dessert, not television, or not something else equally unrelated to the bike. The discipline will have more of an impact on your child if, as in this instance, use of the bike is taken away as opposed to anything else.

Of course, if the misbehavior somehow involves the use of the television, then, that is when the television should be used as part of the discipline. Likewise, if your child misbehaves with his or her computer, then, being consistent, the computer would be part of the disciplinary measure. Got it?

Granted, there will be times when it will be next to impossible to use a specific object as part of the discipline. And, that's OK. All we are saying is that you should get into the habit of using the "misbehaved-with" (our term) object, whenever you can, for maximum effect.

RULE OF THUMB #4

Institute Consequences Immediately

Whenever your child misbehaves, do not waste any time putting the disciplinary consequences into operation. For maximum effect, the discipline should be implemented as soon as possible after the misbehavior occurs. "Wait 'til your father comes home" just won't cut it! The more time that passes after a child misbehaves, the less of an impact the discipline will have.

This is where that preplanning comes in. If you know what disciplinary consequence will follow a particular misbehavior, then you will be in a position to put it into effect immediately. And, as previously noted, when this is done consistently, the misbehavior should diminish significantly and/or be eliminated for good!

RULE OF THUMB #5

Balance

When we speak of balance, we are referring to balancing the punishment with positive reinforcement. With this rule, we are intending positive reinforcement to include statements such as: "You are doing a good job"; "It's nice to see you and your brother playing together without arguing"; or, "It makes me happy to see how nicely you are sharing", and so on. These types of statements should also be accompanied by a hand on the child's shoulder, a hug, or, a LIGHT pat on the back, etc.

At this point, let us tell you that the positive reinforcement would be giving the child something positive, such as one of the aforementioned statements, AND, giving the child this type of reinforcement when he or she IS NOT MAKING A BID FOR IT! We call this "catching the child being good".

For instance, if you have two sons who argue a lot and, one day, you find them playing nicely together, that is the time to make it your business to CASUALLY go into the room, walk up them, put your hands on their shoulders, and, IN A SOFT TONE OF VOICE, tell them how much it pleases you to see them playing quietly together.

Then, quickly get out of the room!

Remember, punishment nor positive reinforcement will work alone. You cannot have all of one and none of the other. Balance is the key for success!

RULE OF THUMB #6

Make the Punishment Fit the Crime

As we proceed through our last, but certainly not least, rule, let us point out that we are using the term "crime" in the loosest possible sense. Obviously, and hopefully, your average children will not be committing any crimes. They will, however, be "committing" some misbehaviors. And, if you've been closely following along, when the misbehavior occurs, the appropriate punishment, or consequence, should immediately be put into operation. Thus, this "punishment fitting the crime" can be reworded into "consequences fitting the misbehavior".

The basic idea here is to not go overboard when disciplining your children. Excess does not lead to success. When deciding on an appropriate punishment, you must keep in mind the degree of severity of the misbehavior. You don't need a sledgehammer to kill a fly. Nor do you need to ground a child for a week because he or she missed one curfew. By using your common sense, good judgment, and the concepts discussed in this book, you should be able to get the hang of making the punishment fit the crime without too much trouble.

OK. These are the five basic rules of thumb that can be applied across the board to further your efforts toward smart parenting. However, before moving on through this book, we would like to add a very important point, or rule, if you will. And, that point is---NO HITTING!

You can accomplish a lot more by using appropriate language and consequences than by physically hitting your children. Remember, children learn what they live. If children frequently experience getting hit, the only thing you are doing is inadvertently teaching your children that violence and aggression are the means to resolving problems and conflicts. And, we are sure you would agree, this is not a lesson that you would want your children to learn.

What you want your children to learn is to use their brains, not their brawn, when difficulties arise. If they learn this lesson, they will have learned a lot!

Chapter 8

PARENTING, PERCEPTIONS, AND OTHER THINGS (*NOT NECESSARILY IN THAT ORDER*)

A s you move along on your journey toward being a smarter and more effective parent, there are, of course, additional considerations that you, as the parent, must be aware of in order to increase the probability of attaining your ultimate goal. So, as you continue reading, which we are sure you will, bear in mind that the ideas described in this chapter---indeed, throughout this book---are to be understood, remembered, and, perhaps most important of all, put into operation, if you are to have any degree of success in managing your children's behavior.

Two of these considerations that we feel should be addressed are the ideas of short-term memory and a child's ability to focus. Needless to say, both of these concepts can have a direct impact on your perceptions (more about perceptions later) of your child's behavior, which, in turn, will directly affect your decision as to whether or not your child may or may not be misbehaving at any given point in time.

Please note that the order of presentation is not to suggest that the first presented is more important than the second nor the second more important than the first. Quite the contrary. Both carry equal importance, and, we might add, they are every bit as important as every other concept mentioned in this volume. Now, since we mentioned short-term memory first, we will deal with short-term memory first.

Briefly stated, short-term memory limits the number of individual items that a person can hold in his or her conscious memory at any given point in time. We all have a limit to the capacity of our short-term memory. However, as might be expected, a very young child's capacity limit is, by nature, more limited than that of an older child or adult.

For example, while we, as adults have a capacity limit of approximately seven separate items (telephone number, anyone?), children younger than seven years of age generally have an item capacity limit that is less than that number. And, the farther below seven years of age that you go, the fewer the number of items that that child can keep in his or her short-term memory at any one time (see "Appendix I" for specific ages and their approximate corresponding short-term memory limits).

As an example, since it is generally believed that the average three year old child has a short-term memory capacity of about two items, we, as adults, cannot expect the three year old to remember more than two commands at a single time. Thus, if a parent tells her three year old child, in rapid succession, to: 1) pick up his toys; 2) shut off his light; and, 3) come to the table for dinner, chances are that one of these commands will be left undone---not because the child is deliberately being disobedient, but, rather, because he just forgot! He just couldn't hold all three commands in his short-term memory.

Thus, in a scenario such as the one just described, it would be normal, or typical, for that three year old to not completely follow-through on all three behavioral commands. And, following from this, that child wouldn't, and shouldn't, be punished for being disobedient when, the fact of the matter is, that child was just acting like an average three year old child would probably act.

Therefore, depending on the age of their young child, it would be wise for parents to limit their successive commands to a number that their child can cognitively handle (again, see "Appendix I").

Speaking of memory, hopefully you will recall that the second item mentioned above referred to a child's ability to focus. More specifically, the child's ability to focus on what is being said to him or her at a specific point in time. In parent-child relations, understanding this idea of the child focusing on what is being said can reduce some of the difficulties that could arise between parents and their children, difficulties that can sometimes lead to the parent thinking that some type of discipline is necessary, when, in reality, it is not a disciplining situation at all!

To further explain, when a young child is engaged in an activity that he or she is focused upon, such as playing with a favorite toy or watching a television program, that child is going to need some time, however brief (and it will be different for different children), in order to REFOCUS, or, reorient himself or herself, thus allowing the child to appropriately switch his or her behavior. Granted, the time needed may be quite minute in the overall scheme of things, but, it is time, nonetheless.

For instance, if a young child is actively involved in some type of play activity, and the parent tells the child to do or to not do something, chances are pretty good that the child may "miss" the first few words of what the parent had just said. Consequently, since the child DID NOT FULLY HEAR what was said by the parent, the child CANNOT FULLY UNDERSTAND what was just said by the parent. And, if neither fully heard nor fully understood, then, how can the child be expected to respond appropriately to the parent's words? The truth is---the child can't!

When this type of scenario plays out in one's home, or elsewhere, the parent would tend to perceive disobedience rather then perceiving a lack of hearing and/or understanding on the part of the child. Needless to say, something like this can definitely create a problem where a problem really doesn't exist. So, what's a parent to do? Well it's so simple that it is very easy to miss.

In trying to refocus your child because you have something that you want to say to the child, it would be a good idea to get into the habit of saying the child's name FIRST and then giving the child a brief amount of time to refocus. Once this is done, then you can continue with whatever you were going to say.

By saying the child's name first, you are giving the child the time that he or she may need in order to refocus from his or her activity to what you are saying. When this is done, you can be reasonably sure that you have the child's full attention, BEFORE you continue to speak.

OK. Now that you have some idea of what the two aforementioned concepts consist of, we can proceed with a few words about a third concept that is necessary in the understanding of your children's behavior. That third concept, which we have been alluding to, is the idea of perception.

Please keep in mind that, when speaking about perception, we are not referring to just SEEING something. That would not be perception. That would, more or less, be sensing.

No. When we speak of perception, we are speaking of actually PERCEIVING something---not just seeing it. Allow us to explain. To put this in brief terms (since this is not a book on perception), to perceive something, anything, means to become aware of (there's that word again! It's beginning to haunt you, isn't it?) and gain a true understanding of whatever it is that is going on in your environment at any given time.

In other words, the perception of something is the understanding of whatever it is that you are sensing from your environment, be it words, behaviors, pictures, feelings, etc.

And, just because we have mentioned sensing, we will tell you that sensing something means that you have become alert to something occurring in your environment, but yet, not fully understanding what that something is. You need your perception to "kick in" in order for the understanding to, hopefully, take over.

On the surface, this appears quite simple enough. However, as with most things in life, there are many factors that enter into the equation that would tend to render the perception process much more complex.

First of all, a person's history can color how he or she perceives something in the present. For example, if a person was taught, as a child, that some behavior was wrong (whether or not it was), and, if that person saw his or her own child engaging in that exact same behavior years later, that parent would probably PERCEIVE the behavior just witnessed as being wrong or bad, or whatever negative adjective you would like to place on the behavior.

On the other hand, a different parent may have been taught, again as a child, that that exact same behavior WAS NOT wrong. If this was the case, then, that second parent would probably tend NOT TO PERCEIVE that behavior, years later, as a problem.

Now, please keep in mind that this difference in the perceptions of the different parents would probably occur regardless of what that particular behavior was, within reason, of course. Putting it another way, the different backgrounds, or "teachings", of the different parents regarding certain types of behaviors, is probably leading to one parent perceiving the behavior as OK while the other parent perceiving that same behavior as not OK.

Make sense? We sure hope so! OK, now let us continue.

Another aspect that must be considered when trying to understand the perceptions of children's behavior, is the issue of the culture within which the parents were raised and the culture within which their children are being raised. More specifically, some behaviors that may be perfectly acceptable in one culture may be completely taboo in another culture. This can pose serious problems when the parents were brought up in a culture that is vastly different from the one in which they are bringing up their own children.

If parents do not understand what is acceptable (again, within reason) in their newly adopted culture, which may have very different customs, values, and attitudes, then, this lack of understanding will, more than likely, have a huge influence on their perceptions of their children's behavior. When this occurs, problems can easily arise with discipline, not to mention problems with their parent-child relationships.

Another aspect that must be addressed relating to an understanding of perception as it pertains to children's behavior, is the style of parenting that is in use in a particular household. That style can, and probably will, alter how the parents are perceiving what it is that their children are doing and saying.

At this point, however, we are going to do one of our favorite things---digress!! We are digressing in order to describe for you the three major types of parenting styles that can be found in today's homes. Granted, as with almost anything else, there will be variations to the three that we will be discussing. Our intent here is for you to understand the overall "gist" of these three most common types.

To begin with, let us discuss the type of parenting referred to as the authoritarian type. When parents "rule" their households---and families---in an authoritarian manner, they will tend to be very rigid parents. And, while rules and regulations in the home are absolutely essential, the rules and regulations set up by authoritarian parents tend to be too extreme. If their children dare to question any of those rules, this type of parent would, more than likely, respond by becoming even more extreme---if that is at all possible!

In short, authoritarian parents do not want any questioning of their rules by their children because they tend to view the questioning as a direct challenge to their authority, authority that they so desperately want to maintain.

In addition to the above, authoritarian parents tend to rule with an "iron fist" and they also tend to make all kinds of unreasonable demands on their children. And, in many instances, their children cannot meet those unreasonable demands because they, the children, are either cognitively and/or physically unable to do so.

Needless to say, authoritarian parents' perceptions of their children's behavior can quite easily be quite far off the mark, so to speak. Much of what they perceive as disobedience is, in reality, an inability on the part of the children to comply, and not a direct refusal to obey. However, it is important to note that, in the beginning, things may start out as an inability to comply, but, in many cases, that inability will probably turn into refusal and generalize across behaviors.

Continuing along this line, please do not get us wrong. Obedience from one's children is a fantastic thing. It is something that most parents strive for. It is probably the main reason you are reading this book. However, the problem with authoritarian parents is that their demands for obedience are, as above, way too extreme.

When authoritarian parents think that they perceive some disobedience---whether real or not---they will punish. And, unfortunately, when this type of parent punishes, the punishment is usually quite punitive, severe, and, in general, not very fair. In short, the punishment definitely does not "fit the crime".

As if the aforementioned characteristics weren't enough, the authoritarian parents also try to control virtually every aspect of their children's lives. Consequently, the children generally do not get any opportunities at home to make decisions; solve problems; learn effective interpersonal skills; or, to put it succinctly, they do not learn how to effectively stand on their own two feet. And, to the level-headed individual, these skills are the very skills, among others, that every child needs to learn in order to effectively function as an adult. Unfortunately, with authoritarian parents, the children will probably have great difficulty acquiring those aforementioned skills.

There are, of course, other characteristics that are hallmarks of the authoritarian parent. But, at this point, we will assume that you have gotten the picture. And, if you think that we are exaggerating this, you are mistaken. This kind of rigid, inflexible, punitive parenting occurs in more homes than you could ever imagine.

Hopefully, you are still with us. Now, continue reading along as we move on to a second type of parenting, which is referred to as the permissive parent. Whereas the previously mentioned authoritarian parents are very, very strict, rigid, and punitive, the permissive parents can be considered to be their opposite.

Specifically, the permissive parents exercise TOO LITTLE control over their children. They tend to be rather loose with whatever rules they may have, if, in fact, they have rules. And, unlike the authoritarian parents, the permissives tend not to punish their children, and, more often than not, they tend to give their children too much independence too early in their lives.

Oops! We forgot to mention something a couple of paragraphs ago. How unlike us! Anyway, we forgot to mention that the authoritarian parents will try to withhold any amount of independence from their children for as long as the parents can possibly withhold it. OK. Now we will return to the permissives.

While permissive parents generally take care of their children's basic needs, close supervision and guidance---very important needs indeed---are, unfortunately, quite minimal. As you can surmise, the permissive parents tend to take a "hands off" approach to parenting. And, in our professional opinion, a "hands off" approach to parenting is never a good thing.

Finally, the third type of parenting style that we shall discuss in this book is the authoritative type. This is the type of parenting that parents should--- again, in our professional opinion---strive for. This is the type of parenting that makes the most sense. And, this is the type of parenting from which children can actually learn some constructive life skills.

Looking more closely at what it means to be an authoritative parent, we can say that the authoritative parents set up rules and regulations and have certain standards that their children must adhere to. However, they are not rigid and the standards they set are generally reasonable and appropriate.

These parents demand that their children work up to their own potential, whatever that potential might be. Contrary to what some may believe, there is absolutely nothing wrong with demanding that your children work and perform up to their own individual potential.

However, unlike the authoritarian parent, the demands of the authoritative parents are usually appropriate, given their children's physical and cognitive abilities. For example, if authoritative parents have a child who has the ability to achieve "A's" in school, these parents want their child to achieve at that level, within reason, of course. On the other hand, if they KNOW that their child's maximum potential will produce mostly "B's" and "C's", then, for these parents, "B's" and "C's" it will be!

In addition, it is important to note that the authoritative parents do value discipline. However, unlike the authoritarian parents, the authoritative parents are not punitive. They do punish their children with consequences, but, the punishment usually tends to "fit the crime". In other words, the punishment/consequences are appropriate---not harsh or extreme.

Another characteristic of the authoritative parents is that they are open to having discussions with their children on matters concerning rules and regulations. Of course, we are speaking of situations that are within certain limits. Common sense and good judgment on the part of the parents are key factors here.

When situations arise that would necessitate a new rule or a change in an already existing rule of the household, authoritative parents will listen to any thoughts that their children may have on the issue at hand. Obviously, the parents will have the final say. But, the point is that, at least, they are open and objective enough to allow for some input from their children.

This action goes a long way toward helping boost the children's self-concept and self-esteem, as well as instilling the feeling that each of them is an important member of the family.

Continuing with our description, authoritative parents generally will allow their children an appropriate amount of independence, given their child's age and cognitive level of development. This, of course, is in direct contrast to the two aforementioned parenting types, with the authoritarian type withholding as much independence as possible and the permissive type usually giving much too much independence at too early an age.

It appears that, for the most part, the relationships between authoritative parents and their children are such that the parents generally will know their children well enough, and hence, be able to determine just how much independence their individual children can successfully handle.

However, we would like to point out that this would be the average scenario, as there are always exceptions, as we have mentioned several times throughout this book. And, again, we want to stress that the child's age and cognitive ability level must be taken into serious consideration by parents when they are doling out independence.

At this juncture, we believe that the issue of independence deserves a side note. If you, as the parents, are deciding on a level of independence to allow one or more of your children, please remember that it is far better to make an error on the side of caution and give less independence than to make the mistake of giving too much independence too soon.

Parents must realize that, once a certain degree of independence is given, it will be extremely difficult---if not, totally impossible---to pull in the reigns and begin to withhold some of that already-given freedom. What you, as the parents, must keep in mind is that you can always increase the amount of independence, even by small increments. But, be aware that you probably will not be able to decrease it without a war breaking out in your household. So, in our professional opinion, why ask for a problem?

The smart thing to do would be to closely observe your child in order to determine the degree of independence that you THINK he or she can adequately handle, and then, give that amount. Once you determine that your child can successfully handle that amount, then, and only then, should you attempt to increase it. As always, you, as the parent, must continuously monitor your child's success in handling whatever amount of independence that you have allowed.

Please note: When discussing issues related to independence with your children, DO NOT succumb to statements such as: "But all my friends are staying out until midnight"; or, "All my friends' parents let them hang out as the mall and the parents go home". Or, how about: "You just want to keep treating me like a baby"; or, our particular favorite, "If you loved me, you would let me_____"(we're sure you can fill in the blank).

If these statements sound familiar, and we thing some of them will, totally disregard them. The one thing that takes precedence is that YOU MUST DO WHAT IS BEST FOR YOUR CHILD---not anyone else's child.

So, there you have it. An admittedly very brief description of the three major types of parenting. Hopefully, you can draw your own sensible conclusions from our discussion. But, just in case, we will remind you that the authoritative parenting style does appear to be the best of the three mentioned. Thus, in our professional opinion, authoritative parenting should be your goal.

And, if you remember nothing else from this chapter, remember that parents must strive to provide warmth for their children; make appropriate demands on them; provide appropriate discipline for their children; be present in their children's lives, both physically and emotionally; and, respond to all of their children's needs.

By this time, you may have forgotten that our discussion of parenting styles was prompted by our explanation of aspects that can influence perceptions. So, let us continue.

One additional aspect to consider in the realm of perceptions is the setting in which a particular behavior occurs. For some parents, this may change their perceptions of the behavior in question.

For example, yelling while watching a baseball game at a stadium would probably be perceived as OK by parents, provided, of course, that the language was kept in the acceptable category. However, that same yelling while sitting at the dinner table or conversing with you, the parent, would, more than likely, be perceived as not being appropriate behavior. Same behavior (yelling)---different circumstances---different perceptions.

OK. Enough about perceptions and behavior. We think you have the idea. Perceptions can and do strongly influence how you, as the parent, will view your children's actions. If you stay grounded in reality, remain aware of what is really going on, and, maintain objectivity, your perceptions should be relatively on target. If your perceptions are realistic and you have appropriate consequences at your disposal, then you will have a great advantage when trying to deal with your children and manage their misbehavior.

And, please do not forget the other concepts mentioned in this chapter: The child's short-term memory; the child's focusing; your refocusing of the child; and, the style of parenting. All of these, and, of course, perception, are vastly important in your attempts at managing---and understanding---your children's behavior.

Chapter 9

MANAGE YOUR TIME – REDUCE YOUR STRESS

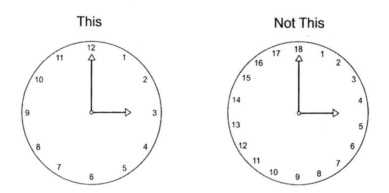

This   Not This

As you continue through this book, you will notice that this chapter, along with the three succeeding chapters, all deal, in one way or another, with the issue of controlling your stress. Now, as you read this, you may be wondering why the issue of stress management is being incorporated into a book on parenting. After all, you picked up this book to learn more about parenting---not about stress.

Well, in response to your probable puzzlement, we will say this. Your children, or, more specifically, your children's misbehavior, can, and probably does, cause you to experience stress. How could it not? And, if you are stressed, you probably will not be thinking as clearly as you normally would; you will, more than likely, be feeling fatigued; your irritability quotient will probably go up; and, your fuse will be significantly shortened.

When you take all this stress-related fall-out into consideration (and we have mentioned only the tip of the iceberg), it is not a giant leap to realize that your overall functioning is not going to be up to par when you are overstressed. And, if your functioning is not up to par due to stress, your interactions with your children can't help but suffer in the process.

So, this is why we have included stress management into a book about parenting. Learn how to effectively manage all aspects of your stress, and, in the final analysis, you should have a better shot at more effectively managing your children.

Now, at this point, before we get into the very significant issues of relaxing and managing your stress, we must first introduce you to the concept of "time-out"---FOR YOURSELF! Now, don't laugh. We are serious about this, and, after you read this chapter, hopefully, you'll also be serious about it.

If you have young children (if you're reading this book, you probably have), you probably know that time-out is used as a technique for attempting to manage the behavior of children. However, in your case as an adult, time-out becomes more of a pleasurable, somewhat self-indulgent activity. Now, believe us when we say that there is absolutely nothing wrong with a little self-indulgence. You may not be used to it, but, there really is nothing wrong with it.

Everyone could use a little self-indulgence from time to time as part of an overall stress management routine. So, as you follow along through the next few pages, we will describe for you how you can begin managing your time in order to work periods of time-out into your own life---hopefully on a daily basis. Now, doesn't that sound great? Of course it does!

REVIEW YOUR DAY

As you try to decide approximately where to insert the periods of time-out into your day, allow us to start you off. To begin with, you need to review what is a typical day for you, as an individual. This is not as easy as it sounds. It can be quite a tedious task. But, it is definitely worth the effort. In fact, it is a must! An Activity-Time Chart, for the purpose of reviewing your day, can be found in Appendix II.

Hopefully, by the time you complete the chart, it will become clear that you probably do have some time to spare during the course of a typical day. However, if, on the other hand, you feel that you don't have any additional time, then it is imperative that you pay close attention to what you are reading and, hopefully, we can take care of that perception.

If you want to eek out some extra time for yourself, then you have to determine how your time is currently being spent during the course of your typical day. Now, please do not jump up and down insisting that none of your days are typical. We can almost guarantee that, when all is said and done, you will discover that you have more typical days than not. So, settle down and stop jumping!

Now, as you are reading these illustrious words, you are probably asking yourself: "How do I accomplish this task? How can I go through an entire day without forgetting something"? These are very natural questions and, over the next few lines (well, maybe a little more than a few), we will tell you about the "how-to's" of this process.

First of all, find a quiet place in your home to sit down to begin your investigation. This area that you choose should also be as free from as many auditory and visual distractions as possible. You do not want to closely review your day's activities with the television blasting or the radio pumping out "metal rhythms". You want this place to be quiet and pleasant. You want the time spent on this activity to be as peaceful as possible.

You should also keep in mind that this quiet place must be physically comfortable for you. If it is comfortable, you will probably be more willing and motivated to spend the necessary time on your project. If you have children, it would probably be a good idea to wait until they are either in school or in bed before you begin your efforts. Also, be sure to have a piece of paper and a pen or a pencil available so you can memorialize on paper what you come up with.

It is so much easier to write things down on paper than to try to keep the information in your head. If not written down, then, when you try to recall the information at a later date, you will invariably forget some or most of whatever it is that you are trying to remember. Unfortunately, many of the things that may be forgotten would be just the items that really needed to be remembered! Isn't this usually the case?

Do we "hear" a question? "Where do I begin, you ask?" Well, that answer is fairly simple. Like anything else, you begin at the beginning. You begin reviewing your typical day from the moment you wake up in the morning, assuming, of course, that you sleep during the night. From that point, you go through the entire day's routine. As recommended above, write down everything that you can think of that occurs during your typical day. To help you along with your efforts, do not forget to use the Activity-Time Chart (again, see Appendix II) as your guide.

When you look at the Activity-Time Chart, you will see that the form is divided into thirty minute blocks of time. We have selected a starting time of 7:00 a.m. and an ending time of 11:00 p.m. The times are listed down the far left-hand margin of the page. Of course, if your typical day begins at a different time, such as 6:00 a.m. or 6:30 a.m., you would simply cross out the printed times and insert the time schedule that would be more appropriate for you. Likewise, if your day begins at 9:00 a.m. or (bless you) 10:00 a.m., then one of these times would be your starting time. Needless to say, the day-ending times would change accordingly.

Remember, even if you change the starting time, you should still keep the time intervals to 30 minutes as in the printed chart. Furthermore, not only is the time to be the most applicable to you, but everything that you enter on the chart is to be what is MOST applicable to you on your typical day. Try not to leave anything out.

Now, we have anticipated that, at this point, some of our readers might still be thinking that they do not have any typical days to work with. They may be thinking that ALL of their days are quite unique. Granted, we generally like to think of each new day as a new beginning, as something unique. But for our purposes here, THINK TYPICAL!

Once you comb through your activities, responsibilities, and interactions, you may, more than likely, come to the conclusion that your days are more typical than you perceive them to be. This does not mean that you are a boring person. It just says that you are like most of us who have more typical days throughout our lives than non-typical days.

So, if you are ready, now is as good a time as any to begin your adventure of discovery!

To begin with, for each block of time, enter the activities that you would perform during those respective time periods. Remember, if your times differ from the printed times, change the times to whatever suits your living pattern or style. To nudge you along and to give you some practice, we will briefly lay out an example for your review. It will help if you have a copy of the Activity/Time Chart in front of you so you can follow along more easily as we describe the steps involved.

Suppose you normally arise at 7:30 a.m. This would be the start of your typical day. Because our pre-printed starting time is actually 7:00 a.m., you would leave the top row empty and begin recording on the second row – the 7:30 a.m. row. If, however, you get up at 6:30 a.m., you can either change the pre-printed times OR you can just add a new row to the top of the chart. This will accomplish the same purpose.

Next, in the "Activity" column, write down everything that you can remember that you normally do during that first half-hour time block. Remember, every activity that you can think of should be put in that time block---no matter how insignificant it may appear to you as you are filling out the form.

Now, before continuing, one note of caution may be very necessary at this point. Please keep in mind that, whatever you do, DO NOT get yourself all stressed out when filling out this chart. The purpose of the task is not to increase your stress, but, hopefully, in the long run, the purpose is to DECREASE your stress! And, also remember, the chart is used for AWARENESS, pure and simple. AWARENESS...NOT STRESS!

So, take your time with it, within reason, of course. If, however, you find yourself getting stressed with this self-reflection, you may turn to the relaxation chapter (Chapter 11) in this book for a sneak preview of some relaxation exercises. You can select one, read about it, and then, try it. Once you are sufficiently calmed down, you can continue with your task of filling out the aforementioned chart.

OK. Now that we've cautioned you, let us continue. Assuming that you have had some time to go through the Activity/Time Chart and have listed your various activities with the corresponding time periods, it is now time to formally move on to the issue of stress. In other words, the time has come to assess your own level of stress during each of the activities in question that you have listed on the chart. In order to accomplish this, you can use the following scale levels which would correspond to the amount of stress that you SUBJECTIVELY feel during the typical situations that you have listed on the chart.

Number	Level of Stress
1	None
2	Mild
3	Moderate
4	Moderate to Severe
5	Severe

For example, if you felt no stress during a particular activity, you would place a check mark in the column labeled #1. If you estimated that you were feeling a mild level of stress, you would then put a check mark in column #2. To continue, if you perceived that you experienced a level of stress that you would describe as being about 50-50, you would mark off column #3, and so on.

Keep in mind that the stress assessment isn't the easiest thing to do. And, you will probably find that, the more activities that you have jammed into a particular block of time, the more stress you probably felt.

When doing this exercise, you will find that the more you assess your stress levels, the more aware you will become. And, the more aware you become, the easier the exercise will be to perform. In fact, you will probably discover that, just making yourself aware of the amount of stress that you are subjectively feeling, may, in and of itself, actually reduce some of that stress in the future! It probably will not happen this way all of the time (nothing happens all of the time), but, at times, it may.

NOTE YOUR STRESSORS

As you go over your Activity/Time Chart, take special note of the level of stress associated with each activity. Needless to say, the higher the number assigned to the particular situation, the more stress you are perceiving. Do not be concerned with whether or not someone else thinks something is stressful. That's not important in this context. What IS important is that, if YOU perceive some event as being stressful, then, for your purposes, IT IS STRESSFUL!!!

If you find that, when you review your chart, you do not always remember, in it's entirety, the specific event or activity associated with a particular stress level that you have entered, then, when you are initially completing your chart, you may need to be more specific in the "activity" column in relating the details. For instance, if one of your stress-related activities was that you "checked the time", instead of just writing, "checked time" under the activity section, you could add a few more delineating words. Specifically, rather than just writing "woke up late", you could put down, "woke up late and I think I am going to be late for work".

By adding these few additional words of explanation, you will be better able to easily refresh your memory when you go back over your chart several days later. And, if you have to use additional pieces of paper to complete the description, then do so. The idea is to be very specific so your recall will be as easy as possible. This way, your awareness (remember that?) and perception of the activity have the best chance of being as realistic and as accurate as possible.

Now, continue along with us through the next chapter as we further explore your Activity-Time Chart.

Chapter 10

ANALYZE YOUR ACTIVITY-TIME CHART

When you have completed your Activity/Time Chart, you will now have, at your fingertips, a concise summary of YOUR typical day. Remember, this is YOUR typical day---not your children's; not your spouse's; not your neighbor's; but, YOUR OWN!

When reviewing the chart, you need to pay very close attention to what you have written down. Follow along as we give some possible solutions for some types of problems that you may find present once you do your review. It should be noted that these types of difficulties are really quite common. So, again, DO NOT get stressed-out! Stress is not the objective---destressing is!

I. TIME ALLOTMENT

As you begin, note how much time you allot yourself for specific activities---especially the routine ones. You may find that you are trying to squeeze too much activity into too little time. If this is the case, you are AUTOMATICALLY "asking for" trouble. In other words, you are setting yourself up for additional stress, and related problems, without even realizing it!

Possible Solutions

1. More Time with Less to Do

One of the easiest solutions for this type of problem would be to allow yourself the luxury of *more time for fewer activities*. Keep in mind, no one is going to hand you time on a silver platter. Nor is anyone---at least not in the foreseeable future---going to add any more hours to your day. Twenty-four hours is, always was, and always will be just that, 24 hours. Twenty-four hours is what you have, and, 24 hours is what you get! No more. No less. That's it! So, learn to comfortably live within those hours.

And, remember, you are probably sleeping for about eight of those 24 hours, give or take a few minutes here and there. So, in the real world, that actually gives you only about 16 hours to work with. Now, we are not trying to add stress to this issue. No, quite the contrary. We are just trying to put your waking hours into the proper perspective.

So, in reviewing what you have been typically doing during your waking hours, try to identify what activities/chores/etc. you can reasonably eliminate. If you scrutinize the items very closely, we could almost guarantee that you will find, at various times during the day, some activities that could be done away with. Then, with this done, you will truly have *more time for fewer activities*.

2. Consolidate

As you review your chart, you may find that some of your activities/chores/etc. during the typical day can be consolidated, thereby HAVING THE EFFECT of giving you the additional time that you may need for your time-out, relaxation, and, stress relief. And, as above, you may be able to eliminate some activities/chores/etc., again resulting in additional time for yourself.

3. Rearrange

Related to, but a little different from, the above idea of consolidation, is the idea of rearranging your activities/chores/etc. Through your travels, you may find that you can rearrange some of your activities/chores thereby allowing for some additional time for yourself. For example, if you want to buy something at a particular store and you also have something else to take care of in the vicinity of that store (groceries, pick up dry-cleaning, etc.), it would probably be a wise move to combine all of these things into one trip instead of two or three trips. If this is done, you'll save some valuable time and, of course, the net result would be more time for yourself. As an added benefit, you will probably also save some money on things such as gasoline or taxi or bus fare.

4. Time is Short: Get Up!

If, after reviewing the chart, you discover that your time actually IS too short, you may have to (sorry!) think about the possibility that you may not be getting up early enough in the morning in relation to what you need to accomplish during the day. Obviously, the first thing you should do in this instance is to figure out just how much additional time you need, and then, start your day with that extra time "built in". If, upon your inspection, you find that you actually need as much as an extra 25 or 30 minutes in your waking day, then you would be smart to plan on getting up 30 to 45 minutes earlier, just to be on the safe side. Again, as above, you will be working in some extra time to devote to yourself for your relaxing and de-stressing---not working in extra time solely for the purpose of cramming in more of the same types of activities/chores that you are supposed to be trying to eliminate and/or consolidate!

II. STRESS LEVEL

Once you have the time factor straightened out, the next thing to do is to go to the "stress level" columns. In reviewing these columns, you should be able to identify which activities correspond to which SUBJECTIVELY determined stress levels. Take particular note of all those "4's" and "5's". Those are the events that are probably creating more stress than you or anyone else needs, and, consequently, those are the activities/chores/etc. that will need your immediate attention.

When this comparison is done with realistic perceptions, you will, more than likely, find that not all of the activities and/or events in your day create the amount of stress that you THINK they create. (This is an added positive effect thrown in for no extra charge!).

To continue, as you review the chart, see if the "3", "4", or "5" level stressors (yes, include the "3's") tended to recur more than once during the typical day. This will give you an indication of where to start in your attempts at reducing your overall stress level.

When confronted with trying to reduce stress, most people would generally begin to eliminate the "5's", work down to the "4's", through the "3's", and, eventually, get as far down as they can through the "2's" and the "1's".

However, please note. You probably will not be able to eliminate all of your stressors. Usually no one can. But, you can try to eliminate as many as possible. Remember, as we have previously noted, everyone is going to have some stress during the course of living in this world. So, why should you be any different?

Possible Solutions

Identify the Importance

As you review the activities and/or events for stress level, you must objectively identify the relative importance and/or necessity of each. As you do this, you may come to the conclusion that:

1. The activities/chores/etc. are not "chiseled in stone";
2. The relative priorities can be changed; and/or,
3. Some of these activities/chores/etc. can be completely eliminated or altered in some way, shape, or form.

When trying to identify relative importance, do not "enshrine" your activities/chores in such a way that they appear to be fixed and inflexible. Indeed, flexibility is the key when considering numbers 1, 2, and, 3, above. Things can and do change. You need to recognize this and use it to your stress-reducing advantage.

Granted, we do realize that some of your daily activities/chores must remain as they are, such as eating meals, getting dressed, going to work, taking care of your children, etc. The point we are trying to get across is that, when doing your review, use your good judgment and common sense to accurately differentiate between those activities/chores that need to remain as they are and the activities/chores that do not. Obviously, it's the ones that do not necessarily need to remain as they are that you can more easily work with.

However, keep in mind that some of your activities/chores that you THINK must remain the same, really can be altered and/or eliminated in some way. We will use #3 to illustrate this point:

If, while on your way to work, you drive some children to school (don't forget your own children), you may want to consider sharing this "wonderful experience" with some of the other parents. In other words, take turns. Even if you go directly past the school on your drive to work, you should not deprive the other parents of this experience! You will be amazed at how a simple adjustment like this could enable you to slow down and actually enjoy your early morning, not to mention, your ride to work.

The bottom line here is to ask yourself: "Is this errand or activity so important that it HAS TO REMAIN as I first listed it"? If your answer to this question is a definite, resounding "NO!", then, use your common sense and good judgment to change the situation in some way so that it is more beneficial for you---timewise, of course!

Now, as we have alluded to above, you probably do not have to be too concerned at the outset with the activities/events with corresponding stress levels of "1" and "2". We all need some palatable amount of stress in our lives. If we had absolutely no stress, we would, more than likely, be dead. Not a pretty picture! As we have been saying, it's those "3's", "4's", and "5's" that require your immediate attention, for these are the stressors that are probably making your life much more difficult than it has to be.

Chapter 11

IT'S TIME TO RELAX!

Ok. Now that you are well on your way to consolidating, rearranging, getting up, and prioritizing, you are now ready for relaxing. Relaxing…It's a joyous, wonderful thing. Having that time for yourself when you can "close out the world", and, if you want, just sit and do absolutely nothing. As we are sure you would agree, many of us would love to relax as much as we could. Many of us would just welcome some free time in our day---however brief---to use for ourselves. (We use the phrase, "many of us" rather than "all of us" because, we are certain that there are some people out there who couldn't care less about whether or not they have time to relax. It's unfortunate, but, nevertheless, it is true. We say this because, in practice, we've come across people who would fit that description.)

OK. Let's continue. As you are probably aware, relaxing is quite important when it comes to our overall well-being. When a person is able to voluntarily bring on a relaxed feeling, that person will, more than likely, feel more in control of what is going on in his or her environment---not to mention, in his or her life! And, feelings of environmental and/or life control generally equals less stress, and, overall, better emotional health. Being able to "bring on" a feeling of relaxation, can, and often does, give a person an "I can handle it" type of attitude, which is a very important attitude to have.

Following from this, if one feels more in control and better equipped to deal effectively with most types of events that would occur in life, then, that person would have one less psychological reason to lose control whenever a challenge arises---like when your children misbehave!

Being able to relax and control yourself will afford you some needed "thinking time" when dealing with your children's behavior. In other words, if you can put relaxation very close to the top of your child-rearing techniques, you will probably be less likely to react impulsively (instead of acting thoughtfully, as you should) to whatever it is your child does or says.

So, for all of you who need some help in learning how to relax (and, who doesn't?), let us, without further ado, get to the art of relaxing.

To begin with, you may or may not know that there are many different relaxation techniques available today. Just go through any number of books on the subject that are available today (but, thankfully, if you are reading this, and you are, you've already made an excellent choice!), and you will read about many relaxation exercises, as well as variations on those exercises, and, still more variations on the variations! However, for our purposes here, which is to help prepare you for being a smart and effective parent, we feel that most of you probably will, more than likely, benefit from some of the simplest---yet effective-- relaxation exercises available. So, take careful note as you read the next few pages.

The relaxation exercises that we will focus on in this chapter include, but may not be limited to:

1. Deep breathing
2. Meditation
3. Visualization
4. Projected imagery

However, prior to continuing with the aforementioned techniques, we would like to point out that, before a person begins learning how to relax, one must learn how to breathe correctly. In our professional opinion, correct breathing is the very basis for feeling relaxed. Indeed, we are quite sure that you are already aware of the fact that breathing is at the basis of life itself! (OK…water and food, too. But, we are not talking water and food here, folks. We are talking breathing!) Obviously, if you can't breathe, then you will not survive. We think you will agree with us on this.

But, to get down to specifics, there is breathing, and then, there is BREATHING. In other words, there is an incorrect manner of breathing as well as a correct manner of breathing, both of which, fortunately, will keep you alive (along with the aforementioned water and food). Obviously, as if you haven't already guessed, in this chapter, we are going to focus on the correct form of breathing.

OK. As you are standing in the bookstore or sitting in your living room thumbing through this book, you are probably thinking: "What are these two talking about! I breathe. I've been breathing my entire life! If I wasn't breathing, I wouldn't be here, and, if I wasn't here, I wouldn't be reading through this wonderful book because I wouldn't be breathing in the first place! What in the world are these two saying"!

Well, we can understand your possible confusion, so, give us a minute or two (depending on how quickly you read), and we will tell you what we are talking about. Fair enough? Fair enough.

We will start by explaining to you how a person breathes incorrectly. Then, we will fill you in on what is generally accepted as a more correct style of breathing. And, in keeping with the theme of this chapter, we might add that this more correct style of breathing is, in fact, a more relaxed style of breathing. So, here we go!

INCORRECT BREATHING

Judging from what we have seen during the course of our work with relaxation training and stress management (not to mention, parenting), it is probably a safe bet to say that many people breathe in an incorrect manner. By breathing incorrectly, we mean breathing with and/or from one's chest. To be more specific, as this type of breather inhales, the chest greatly expands and the shoulders tend to rise upward toward the person's ears. Conversely, when exhaling, the chest collapses and the shoulders return to their usual position.

However, as indicated by the title of this section, this type of breathing is not the most beneficial. Nor is it the most efficient or the most relaxing way to breathe. In general terms, this type of breathing is called chest breathing, and, by it's very nature, chest breathing tends to be a more anxious, and hence, a less relaxed form of breathing.

Now, do any of you parents recognize yourselves? Whether you do or not, you will see what we mean in just a few short minutes---provided, of course, that you continue reading this chapter.

So, we will continue. When breathing with what we call, chest breathing, some things almost always occur. For instance, the person in question usually does not feel as if he or she really took in an appropriate amount of air with relative ease. That person may even find that some tiredness and/or weakness can occur. Additionally, with incorrect breathing, the person may also feel less energetic and less motivated to engage in activities---favorite or otherwise. At times, he or she may even feel a bit light-headed from this shallow type of breathing.

Why is this the case, you wonder? Well, you see, with this shallow, chest breathing, the brain may not be getting a sufficient amount of oxygen to function at it's optimal level. Consequently, it can slow down, so to speak. This, in turn, would have the effect of slowing down the whole system, which, of course, we know as "the person".

Furthermore, when a person breathes from the chest, as previously described, the person would tend to be, in many instances, somewhat tense, anxious, and, more than likely, feeling stressed. This may be a chronic, or continuous state of being, or, it may only occur periodically. In fact, the person may not even make the connection between what he or she is feeling and how he or she is breathing. But, regardless of the level of awareness, that connection exists.

The bottom line is that the overall feeling is definitely not as comfortable or relaxed as it could, or should, be. Needless to say, this type of incorrect breathing is something that any reasonable person would want to avoid and not gravitate toward.

So, with all this in mind, what do you do? You will read the next section---THAT'S what you'll do! And, after reading, you will have discovered one of the key ingredients for feeling calmer and less stressed. And, following from this, when you are calmer and less stressed, you should then have a higher probability of more effectively dealing with whatever life may throw your way---including, but not limited to, your children's misbehavior!

However, a word (or two) of caution appears to be warranted at this time. It is a fact that the symptoms listed above, i.e., tiredness, weakness, feeling light-headed, etc., can also be symptoms of some type of psychological and/or medical problem. Consequently, as we always advise, if you are experiencing these or similar symptoms, we strongly recommend that you immediately consult with the appropriate professional (family physician, licensed psychologist, or licensed psychiatrist) in order to receive an examination. This will hopefully determine if you do, in fact, have a condition or illness that needs some type of treatment over and above that of relaxation training.

CORRECT BREATHING

OK. Now that you, hopefully, have learned what incorrect breathing is like, we will outline for you the process of breathing correctly. Makes sense, doesn't it? Of course, it does!

However, before continuing, permit us to first give you some biological background on this subject of breathing. But, please remember. We are not physicians, nor biologists, nor experts on the respiratory system. So, this brief outline of the biology of breathing is going to be just that---a brief outline. So, here we go!

Breathing does not begin and end with the lungs. That's right! You read that correctly. Obviously, the lungs are used and are an integral part of the breathing process. But, the lungs do not initiate the breathing process. In basic terms, the signal to take a breath comes from the medulla oblongata (how do you like that!), which is located at the base of the brain. The medulla oblongata does not "tell" the lungs directly to inhale or to exhale. Instead, the medulla oblongata actually signals the diaphragm that the body is in need of a breath of air. For those of you who want to know, the diaphragm lies just below the lungs---a very smart place to put it, don't. you think?

To continue. When the diaphragm receives the signal from the medulla oblongata to breathe, the diaphragm contracts thereby allowing the lungs room to expand. As a result of this remarkable occurrence, a person can inhale. Next, when a person is ready to exhale, which, hopefully, is reasonably quick, the diaphragm returns to it's normal position and the lungs contract, thus allowing for the person to exhale.

If the diaphragm was static and did not move, then the lungs would follow suit and not move. Hence, no breathing would take place. Obviously, we would not want this situation to occur---it really would not be in our best interests.

Following this admittedly simplistic view of the respiratory system, we think you will realize that it is the diaphragm that must be controlled---and not the lungs directly---in order to control your breathing. And, if you control your breathing by controlling your diaphragm, then, more than likely, you will be breathing correctly. And, following from this, if you are breathing correctly, you are then on your way to more relaxed and less stressed living.

Keep in mind that, when you breathe correctly, your stomach area should expand for inhaling, accompanied by a much more SUBTLE expansion of the chest. During this process, your shoulders should not be rising toward your ears in any exaggerated manner. Then, as you exhale, the opposite would occur. Specifically, your stomach area should contract, or flatten out, thereby returning to where it was when you began to inhale.

Needless to say, all of this happens with ultra-split-second timing. When all is said and done, you are probably not even aware of what is actually going on when you take those all-important breaths.

Of course, when you become stressed-out and/or anxious, that is the time when you will probably become much more aware of how you are breathing and how your breathing is being affected by the perceived stress. When very stressed and/or anxious, your breathing is usually the first thing to noticeably change. And, being parents, we do not have to tell you that, once you become parents, your lives noticeably change and there is a distinct tendency to become more stressed and/or anxious.

Now, keeping all of the aforementioned information in mind, you can put the process of diaphragmatic breathing into action by using the following helpful steps:

1. Lie down on a bed or sofa, or sit in a comfortable easy chair.
2. Place your hands on your stomach, but, DO NOT press down. Just rest your
   hands lightly.
3. Take in a slow, deep breath, making sure that, as you inhale, your stomach rises.
   As you inhale, slowly and silently count from one to five (about five seconds).
4. Next, hold your breath for a count of two (about two seconds).
5. Then, as you slowly exhale, make sure your stomach is slowly going down.
   As in #3, slowly count from one to five while exhaling (again, about five seconds).

There! That's all there is to it!

One tip to make this procedure a bit easier. While you are doing this exercise, close your eyes and try to imagine that your hands are actually "pushing" the air down from your chest and into your diaphragm.

Now, we know that this all sounds so simple. But, the fact of the matter is that most people who are not accustomed to breathing in this correct manner, do have some difficulty, at first, with this procedure. That said, please do not approach this exercise with a negative or defeatist attitude. You should be ready to accept the fact that you, too, may have some difficulty.

Following from this, you should also keep in mind that you will probably not become an "expert" in this correct breathing process after just one or two attempts. All we can say is to just persevere and, eventually, you will get the hang of it.

Please note that, for best results, it is usually recommended that you practice this exercise four times per day---until it feels natural and is done with relative ease. One other note: Before beginning ANY type of breathing and/or physical exercise, the ones in this book included, it is recommended that you first speak with your physician to get his or her clearance for you to proceed.

One other note of caution appears to be worth mentioning here. After several sequential minutes of deep breathing, prior to getting up on your feet, wait several more minutes to give your breathing a chance to return to what is a "normal" rate for you. Then, when you feel ready, get up very slowly (whether from a sitting or reclining position), and resume your normal activities. However, if you still feel somewhat lightheaded, you should immediately sit down to give yourself additional time to recoup.

Remember, to make the switch from chest breathing to diaphragmic breathing a little easier, you may close your eyes and visualize your hands "pushing" the air out of your chest and into your diaphragm or stomach region. In the course of our work, we have found that this technique of adding the "visual" prompt, had been just the thing some people needed to master this skill of diaphragmic breathing.

Once you have this proper breathing technique mastered, you will find that it can be easily modified into a "full-fledged" relaxation exercise. The following steps show how this can be done.

1. Lie down on a bed or sofa, or sit in a comfortable chair, such as a recliner, and close your eyes.
2. Get into your correct, diaphragmic breathing mode.
3. Next, take in a slow, deep breath while slowly counting to five. This should be done at the rate of about one number per second.

4. When you get to number five, hold your breath for a count of two (about two seconds). Note: Your stomach should be extended at this point.

5. Then after holding your breath for about two seconds, slowly exhale while silently counting backwards from five down to one. Remember, exhale slightly slower than you inhaled.

6. As soon as you silently say the number one, AUDIBLY WHISPER a word beginning with a "breathy H" sound, such as heart, help, heaven, home, and so on. When doing this, make sure that you emphasize the "H" sound of the word that you choose to use. Now, bear with us because this "breathy H" is hard to put on paper. But, here it goes: Hhhhheart; hhhhhelp; hhhhheaven; and so forth. We think you get the idea. This action will have the effect
of "emptying out" all of the stale air left in your lungs.

7. Repeat steps 3 through 6 for approximately five minutes---give or take a minute.

8. Again, once the exercise is completed, give yourself enough time to allow your breathing to return to it's "normal", non-deep breathing mode---the rate that is "right" for you.

9. Now, open your eyes and reorient yourself to your surroundings. Then, get up very slowly. As before, if you feel a little light-headed, sit/lie back down for a few minutes until you are really ready to get up and resume your routine.

Once you have become familiar with the above relaxation exercise, some variation can be added, which we will call "active visualization". However, it should again be noted that, as with any relaxation exercise, it will take different people different lengths of time to master a particular exercise in order to maximize the benefits. As above, all we can say is to persevere and do not get discouraged.

To continue. In order to work with the visualization aspect of a relaxation exercise, there is a step that needs to be taken prior to the nine steps outlined above. And, if we might add, when doing this prerequisite activity, do not get too cute. Just stick with what you know and with what you have experienced in some form.

Obviously, prior to starting the visualization aspect, you need something to visualize. So, just sit quietly and take some time to think of a place that has always been special to you. It should be a place that evokes feelings of calmness, serenity, and peacefulness.

In practice, we have found that some people imagine themselves walking through a garden filled with beautiful, colorful, fragrant flowers. Others imagine themselves sitting on a beach listening to the water splashing against the shoreline. Still others may picture themselves on a mountaintop, or rowing a boat on a calm lake, or being on a tropical island, or walking through a quiet forest, and so on.

As you can see, this selection process is very, very individual. What is calming and peaceful for one person may create some type of anxiety and stress for another. You alone would be the best judge as to what types of environments tend to help you feel calm and relaxed and what types of environments tend to have the opposite effect. So, you need to make that call!

The point of all this is to tell you that, prior to starting this particular relaxation exercise using visualization, think about those places you have been to, or places you may have read about, or, perhaps, places you have seen in movies or on television. Then, just select a setting that you think would meet the criteria of being attractive, calm, peaceful, and, above all, relaxing.

As an aid, and, for future use, you can write down a brief description of this place just below these words.

Relaxing
Place:_____

_____

_____

_____

_____

_____

OK! Since you probably now have a general idea of what we have been explaining to you, you are now in a position to try this visualization exercise.

1. Get comfortable and repeat the deep breathing steps, one through five, as previously outlined.
2. With your eyes closed, allow your breathing rate to naturally return to what is "normal" for you.

3. Now, keeping your eyes closed, build a VERY DETAILED picture in your mind of that very special favorite place that you have chosen to concentrate upon. Visualize the scene growing and growing, becoming more and more vibrant and real. You can accomplish this by describing the scene to yourself---again, in great detail---as if you were describing the scene to someone who has never seen that particular place.

4. Once the image is set in your mind, so to speak, place yourself in the scene. For example, if your place is at the beach, then, picture yourself lying on that beach. While you do this, add all those things to the picture that you would normally see at the beach, such as sea gulls, sailboats, the sand, the waves, the sun, and so forth.

5. Now, for approximately eight to ten minutes, stay with the scene and actually see yourself smiling and enjoying the peace and serenity of the location.

6. When you feel very relaxed, "erase" the picture from your mind, and, with your eyes still closed and mind clear and relaxed, return to concentrating on your breathing for about sixty seconds.

7. When feeling relaxed and breathing normally, slowly open your eyes, get yourself reoriented to your surroundings, and then, SLOWLY get up. As always, lie or sit down again if you feel light-headed and need to regain your composure.

Note: The eight to ten minutes mentioned in #5 above, is only a guideline.

You may want to take some additional time, or, if necessary, you may have to lessen the time. The important thing here is to take enough time to feel relaxed at the conclusion of the exercise. However, a relaxation session should be no more than twenty to thirty minutes in length.

In addition to the aforementioned exercises for deep breathing and overall relaxation, there are other methods that can be employed to achieve a relaxed feeling. For instance, depending on your beliefs, instead of using the calming scene as above (the beach), at step #3, you can meditate with some private prayer. You may also deeply focus on a religious figure, or, on a higher power that would be to your choosing. In addition, a person can also use a biblical passage that has been memorized or a passage from a book dealing with love and/or nature.

As you can see, the image or images that you choose to focus upon is entirely up to you. However, if you find that the image/scene that you originally selected, is not doing the job, then, as you might have guessed, you should rethink that image/scene and change it to something more appropriate for your purposes.

Then, after meditating or doing one of the things mentioned in the previous paragraphs to feel relaxed, return to steps #6 and #7, and proceed as discussed above.

To continue with our quest for relaxation, another exercise that also uses a type of visualization is called projected imagery. The basic idea with this type of exercise is to actually "see" yourself having already accomplished your goal---whatever that goal might be. And, of course, if you are reading this chapter, your goal is to become relaxed.

Putting that goal in terms of projected imagery, your goal is to see yourself as being less stressed and more relaxed. Of course, as we have been saying (or writing?), if you feel less stressed and more relaxed, you should be able to deal more effectively with life, in general, and, more specifically, with your children---assuming, of course, that you also utilize the other information given in this book.

At this time, we will outline for you the procedure for the projected imagery relaxation technique.

1. Repeat the deep breathing steps #1 through #5, until you begin to feel calmer and more relaxed.
2. With your eyes closed, allow your breathing to return to what is "normal" for you.
3. As in the previously described exercise, build a very detailed picture in your mind of your favorite, peaceful place.
4. Then, put yourself directly into the scene and visualize yourself actively enjoying that favorite, peaceful place.
5. Once that picture is firmly in your mind, project yourself six months into the future. Focus on the happy, calm, peaceful, and relaxed look on your face.
6. As you watch yourself enjoying your favorite place, try to "cement" this picture

in your mind of how happy and relaxed you should be feeling in six months. Stay with this picture for about eight to ten minutes. While doing this, make sure that you are breathing easily and gently, in a nice, relaxed manner.

7. When feeling completely relaxed, you can then "erase" the image from your mind as you continue to breathe easily and gently.

8. Open your eyes, get reoriented to your surroundings, and then SLOWLY get up. Again, as we have stated numerous times, if you feel light-headed, sit or lie down again until you can regain your composure.

Well, by this time, we think that you have probably gotten the idea of what a relaxation exercise is. We hope that you have also gotten the idea of how a relaxation exercise can be varied to suit your individual needs. However, there is one thing that we want to emphasize. You must be patient with yourself and allow yourself the time to learn how to do relaxation exercises---not to mention the correct breathing technique. As we have noted, and noted, above, you will not be able to successfully complete these techniques the first few times that you attempt to do them. Like with anything else worth while, you will have to practice. There really is no other way to master these exercises.

It is generally suggested that, in order to be effective, a relaxation exercise should be practiced at least four times per day for at least the first two to three weeks. It would also be best if the four practice periods were spread throughout the course of your day. With commitment, practice, and perseverance, it should not be long before you can get directly into a relaxation mode. And, once you really KNOW what being truly relaxed actually feels like, you could get to the point where you can achieve that nice, calm, relaxed feeling by just taking a few good, deep breaths (from the diaphragm!), and saying to yourself: "I can be calm…I can be relaxed…I am in control of how I feel!"

This last statement is very important, and, when taken to heart, the words can get you through many situations---whether dealing with your children or with some other type of stressful event. You must remember that YOU ARE IN CONTROL of how you feel. What is going on around you SHOULD NOT be in control of you!

Chapter 12

MANAGING YOUR STRESS

OK. Now that you have gone through your typical day and identified various levels of stress; learned correct breathing; and, digested various relaxation exercises, it is now time for us to suggest some additional ways to control your stress. And, as we have said so many times throughout this book, if you can control your stress, you will be in a better position to be a smarter and more effective parent when dealing with your children.

One of the most important things a person needs to learn in this life is how to manage his or her overall stress. And, as parents, it becomes particularly important, especially when considering the two following facts: 1) that you are in a unique position to teach your children how to handle stress; and, 2) that, (as previously stated) if you are handling stress more efficiently, it will be easier for you to think about what you need to think about in order to smartly and effectively manage your children's behavior..

Now, keep in mind that WE ALL experience stress to one degree or another. And, as noted elsewhere in this book, if there was absolutely no stress in your life, you would probably be dead! Due to it's importance and the significant negative effects stress can have on your life, we concluded (using our good decision-making skills!) that we would devote additional space to this topic.

So, in this chapter, we will give a brief overview of some additional ways that may help you to better manage your stress. And, as we have said above, if your stress is managed more effectively, your children's minor infractions will not seem so monumental!

STRATEGIES

I. ONE WAY TO HELP REDUCE YOUR STRESS IS TO ELIMINATE, AS MUCH AS POSSIBLE, ALL THE "MUSTS", "SHOULDS", "HAVE TO'S", "GOT TO'S", "OUGHTS", AND SO ON, FROM YOUR VOCABULARY AND FROM YOUR LIFE.

These types of self-statements *automatically* imply some sense of urgency---even when the situation is far from urgent. And, when this occurs, you will generally feel unnecessarily rushed and stressed. If you use these words with your children, the same implications would apply.

These words, and others like them, are really saying that, whatever it is that you feel you "must do", is the most important thing in your world at that particular time.

Then, if you ARE NOT able to do the specific thing or activity at the moment that you BELIEVE you must do it, you will, more than likely, feel guilty, annoyed, negligent, and, irresponsible.

Needless to say, these emotional reactions would, in turn, create and/or contribute to a great deal of stress in your life---stress that, dare we say, you do not need! And, following from this, if you tend to deal with stress by yelling at your kids, which many parents tend to do, what do you think you would do during these emotionally charged times? You would probably either browbeat yourself and/or hammer away at your children. In our professional opinion, neither of these actions is acceptable.

POSSIBLE SOLUTION

Replace all those aforementioned words and statements, and others like them, with words that would help to eliminate that sense of urgency. You would want to do this because, in most instances, no actual urgency exists. By making this change, you will help yourself get rid of that feeling of being rushed and pressured. This change would also have the effect of reducing and/or eliminating the stress reaction that was associated with these types of non-urgent situations.

Perhaps, at this point, an example will help to clarify this idea for you. Follow closely as we proceed. Instead of saying to yourself: "I *have to* vacuum the whole house when I get home from work today", you can take the implied urgency out of this by changing the statement to something like: "It *would be nice* if I could get to the vacuuming today when I get home from work. But, if I can't---I can't! And, that's OK too! Tomorrow will be here soon enough!"

As you can see, just by changing the "have to" to "would be nice if", takes all of that inappropriate importance and urgency out of the situation of vacuuming. (Of course, if you haven't vacuumed in a really long time, perhaps something else needs to be looked at.) This simple elimination of the urgency takes the stress out of the relatively benign activity of vacuuming. Consequently, you will probably feel much less pressured, less stressed, and, most importantly, more relaxed. Got it? If not, please re-read the paragraph several more times until you do understand the concept.

Granted, it will take some practice to get into the habit of altering your stress producing vocabulary and replacing it with a more relaxed, less stress producing vocabulary. But, once you get the hang of it, you will be amazed at how differently you will feel. And, as an added bonus, your children may pick up on the change in how you feel. You will also be amazed at how much better and more in control you will come to feel, once you have your stress inducing vocabulary under control.

Just in case you need some help in developing that "kinder" vocabulary, just keep reading for more examples. We are sure you can fill in the blanks for yourself with situations that pertain directly to you and your life.

Examples:

1."It would be nice if….."
NOT: "I HAVE TO DO….."
2."There are just so many hours in a day….."
NOT: "I HAVE TO squeeze this in somehow, TODAY!"
3."It would be a good idea to (fill this in yourself), but, if I can't get to it today, that's OK".
NOT: "I've GOT TO get to (whatever), and I better get to it today"!

4. "I'd like to do (whatever) today, but, if I don't have the time, there is always tomorrow"!
NOT: "I OUGHT TO (whatever) today, even if I'm pressed for time. It's GOT TO get done"!

Needless to say, in cases of true emergencies, the above does not apply. The emergency must be taken care of immediately. Also, there are some things that really cannot be put off for another day, such as a project that is due the following day. Something like this would really need to be done. (Maybe the answer here is to not wait until the last minute to finish projects with a deadline. That, alone, can reduce your stress!)

But, the moral of the story is this...Give yourself time and stop making non-urgent situations appear urgent. In the long run, you will feel better and become less stressed. Also, stop looking at your usual activities from the "have to" perspective and begin looking at them from an "it would be nice if" perspective.

II. A SECOND STRATEGY FOR MANAGING YOUR STRESS WOULD BE TO REVIEW YOUR DAILY ACTIVITIES TO DETERMINE IF YOU ALLOW YOURSELF THE LUXURY OF SOME SELF-INDULGENT TIME DURING THE COURSE OF THE DAY. IF YOU DO, FINE. HOWEVER, IF YOU, LIKE MANY PEOPLE, DO NOT, YOU ARE FLIRTING WITH UNNECESSARY STRESS AND PRESSURE.

POSSIBLE SOLUTION

Learn how to work periods of "time-out" into your everyday schedule. As you may recall, we briefly touched upon "time-out" for yourself back in Chapter 9, At this point, we will take some time to more fully explain this concept and it's relationship to controlling your stress.

You may be familiar with this concept of "time-out" if you have children who periodically misbehave. And, which children don't! If you are a teacher of fairly young children, you, too, will probably be familiar with this technique, as used as a disciplinary tool. But, you can also use this same technique as an adult. Yes. And, it's really quite simple to do.

In a nutshell (very professional term, don't you think?), the purpose of the "time-out" strategy is to enable one to feel better and more relaxed by temporarily being removed from the situation that appears to be causing the current problem and the accompanying stress. In the case of children, it is presumed that the situation, within which the child finds himself or herself, is somehow precipitating the stress that the child is feeling. And, it is further presumed that this stress is somehow causing the misbehavior that is being exhibited. So, consequently, the child is removed, or "timed-out" from that situation.

Theoretically, remove the child from the volatile situation or environment, and his or her emotional state should improve. Following from this, the child's behavior should also improve. Over time, the child should ultimately feel better, feel less stressed, and, behave in a more appropriate manner.

Putting this in terms of stress management for yourself, as an adult, does not take much in the way of alteration. During the course of the typical day, many things usually occur that would create stress of one type or another. So, just as the child is removed from the stressful environmental situation, so too can you temporarily remove yourself from your stressful environmental situation.

How do you do this, you ask? Well, you do this by allowing yourself some breathing space. In other words, you "time yourself out" of the situation. Just as with the child, you will probably feel better, less stressed, and, you will, more than likely, be able to think more clearly after your brief respite. In effect, you will be allowing yourself time to tune out the world in order to collect your thoughts (and nerves).

Of course, please keep in mind that, if you have young children that need the presence of an adult, you will have to make arrangements for the "time-out" when another adult is available to look after the youngsters. But, do not despair. These glitches can usually be worked out with a little additional thought and planning. Here's how to get started on your quest for some "time-out".

In order to get some time for yourself for your own "time-out", you will probably have to return to your Activity-Time Chart (see Appendix II) on which you will find your typical day. Hopefully, by the time you are reading these words, you would have already eeked out the time periods for relaxation that we previously spoke about in Chapter 10. But, just in case you haven't, we will go through it again, but, with a slightly different slant.

Now, with chart in hand, go over the blocks of time that you filled in and find yourself ten minutes, or a few more, if you can, at the start of the day. Next, find yourself ten (or more) additional minutes at the end of the day. Once you have both ends of the day covered, find two more ten minute (or more) blocks of time at two other times during the course of the day.

If, after reviewing your chart and doing whatever you had to do to make your use of time more efficient, you still find that you do not have any time to spare (too stressed, maybe???), you might want to try waking up and GETTING OUT OF BED ten or fifteen minutes earlier than you normally do. We mentioned this before but we thing it bears repeating. And, in case you haven't guessed, this action will take care of the first daily "time-out"/stress reduction/relaxation period.

Then, going to the other end of the day, make up your mind to try to end your day ten or fifteen minutes later than you do now. This will automatically take care of the nighttime "time-out"/stress reduction/relaxation period. As a side benefit, this nighttime period can have the advantage of helping you to wind down from your daily activities.

So, if you are keeping count, this takes care of two of the four "time-out" periods. Do we hear you asking what you can do to build in the remaining two periods for stress management? We hope so! However, keep in mind that these two remaining time periods are usually the two that present the most challenge to work in because of other commitments.

These commitments may include your employment, child care, school, and so on. But, when you consider the fact that you really only have to find a TOTAL of another twenty minutes (10 and 10) out of a possible twelve hours, the task does not seem so daunting or impossible.

Now, if you look very closely and carefully at your daily routine, as per your chart, you will probably find the time to "time-out" yourself. During a morning break, during lunchtime, between errands, or, after dinner, are just a few suggestions. But, as we have said previously, you know your schedule best, and, with some thought, we are sure that you can find the time you need to arrange for all four "time-out" sessions.

There is another point that we feel is important to mention right about here, a point especially relevant to stressed-out people. Do not get yourself locked in and become extremely rigid with the time of day that you time yourself out. This, in itself, will create stress. Remember, you do not have to "time-out" at the exact moment each and every day.

Sure, *it would be nice* (remember?) to keep the time factor as steady as possible and as close as possible to your originally selected time. But, remember, life is not predictable. And, because life is not predictable, it would follow that your use of time will not always be predictable.

But, do not despair. If you cannot keep the time the same each day, don't get all worked up about it. On those days when the times must be altered, alter them! But, DO NOT eliminate them!

REMEMBER....REMEMBER....REMEMBER....REMEMBER....
REMEMBER
YOU HAVE TO TAKE THE TIME FOR YOURSELF. NO ONE IS
GOING TO HAND YOU, ON A SILVER PLATTER, AT LEAST 40
MINUTES EACH DAY THAT YOU CAN CALL ALL YOUR OWN!
TAKING THE TIME FOR YOURSELF IS NOT SELFISHNESS---IT
IS CALLED MANAGING STRESS AND KEEPING YOURSELF
TOGETHER!

OK. Let's continue. Once you establish your "time-out" blocks of time, you need to decide what you are going to do for yourself with each block of time that you set aside. Remember, as we previously stated, ten minutes is your starting point. You may be fortunate enough to have fifteen or twenty minutes for some or all of your stress management periods. If you have more than the minimum ten minutes, take them! It would be great and you'll feel great!

At this point, we want to tell you that each of the four "time-out" periods do not have to be the same length of time nor do you have to do the same exact thing with each block of time that you have set aside. For instance, you can start the day and end the day with fifteen or twenty minutes. Then, during the midday when time constraints are usually most demanding, you can insert the remaining two periods for ten or twelve minutes each. The bottom line here is to do what suits you and your schedule best, within guidelines and within reason, of course.

Now, back to: "What do I do during these stress management or empty periods of time"? Our first response to this is that these are not empty periods of time. These are four little gifts that you are giving to yourself to help manage your stress, improve your lifestyle, and hopefully, deal more effectively with your children. So, with this in mind, there are a number of different things that you can do for yourself with your newfound time.

As stated elsewhere in this book, you can do relaxation exercises and/or meditate. You can also begin reading that new novel that has been sitting on the shelf. Or, you can play some type of word and/or puzzle computer game, such as Bookworm or Bejeweled. Yes, you read that correctly! Believe it or not, these types of word and/or puzzle computer games can help reduce your subjective feelings of stress and help you feel more relaxed. (Just as an aside, these types of computer games can also help improve some important cognitive functioning skills.)

In addition to the above, you can read a Bible passage or two, or, you can just sit quietly and enjoy all the wonderful the silence.

There are many, many things that you can find to do during these time periods. And, since you know yourself better than we do, there are probably other ways that you can find to use the time that we would never have thought of.

As you know, there are usually two sides to every coin and story (oops! That's three sides to every story, sorry.), and, this is no exception. Along with what you could be doing, there are also things that you really should avoid doing during these times when you are trying to relax and manage your stress.

DO NOT throw that load of wash into the washing machine, thinking: "I'll get some wash done while I meditate". DO NOT wash and/or dry the dishes. DO NOT vacuum the house. DO NOT dust. DO NOT wash and/or wax and/or vacuum the car. Do you get the picture? We certainly hope that you do. We hope that these few examples of what not to do will help you not to do them!

A good rule of thumb would be this: Do not do anything during the "time-out" periods that the clear-thinking person would consider to be some type of work or chore. Just learn to relax and enjoy the self-indulgence of some leisure time. You've earned it, especially when you have children to raise!

III. A THIRD STRATEGY TO HELP MANAGE STRESS IS TO LEARN HOW TO EFFECTIVELY SOLVE YOUR PROBLEMS

In our fast-paced world, many people do not take the time needed to effectively resolve their serious and not-so-serious problems. They may THINK they are solving their problems, but, they may be reacting emotionally and, as the saying goes, only "putting a band-aid" on the problem situation.

When this is done, you are, in effect, only putting the problem on the back burner, so to speak, to sit there and simmer. If this is how you attempt to resolve problems, the problem will usually resurface at some future time, and, in many instances, the problem becomes even worse than it was originally.

Granted, some situations that you consider to be problems can be put aside to be taken care of at a future time. Only you can be the judge of this. However, our purpose here is to outline a problem-solving strategy that may be useful for you to use when it is time to deal with problem "X", "Y", or, "Z". But, keep in mind that, unresolved, "back-burner" types of problems can create undue stress. So, choose those "back-burner" problems very carefully.

Now, with that said, let's get to the issue at hand, namely, problem-solving. Keep in mind that we are not presenting the only strategy that exists, but, it is one that we have found to be particularly effective with clientele. Follow along as we outline the steps to effective problem-solving:

1. Identify the problem;
2. Generate alternative courses of action;
3. Select an alternative to act on;
4. Act on that alternative;
5. Review the effects of your choice of action; and,
6. If the alternative selected worked, great. But, if it did not work, i.e., solve
   the problem, then you need to return to step #2 and continue, as above, through
   step #6.

Let us now take each of the above steps and explain them in more detail.

1. Identify the Problem

Hopefully, most of you would know when you have a problem to resolve. Granted, there are some people who wouldn't know a problem existed if it hit them on the head. But, we do hope these types of people are few in number. Eventually, for most, if they do not recognize that they have a problem, someone, at some point in time, will probably, and diplomatically, tell him or her: "Hey, do you know that you have a problem"?

If a person is wise and the speaker is trustworthy, he or she will take that notice in the spirit in which it is given. Then, the person could set out to do something positive about the particular problem in question.

If you take stock, so to speak, you will probably find that some of your problems are relatively small and/or may have occurred previously, or something similar may have occurred previously. In these instances, what do you do? You learn from the past, that's what you do! You would use the same or a similar strategy to take care of the current problem, that is, of course, if the previous strategy worked!

It would be nice if, once you took care of a problem, it would go away forever. Fortunately, some problems are like that. But, unfortunately, this is not always the case. More often than not, the problems we experience have some relationship to past difficulties that had not been dealt with effectively. After all, this is not a perfect world and problems (or similar problems) do tend to recur.

As we have noted above, when you feel that you are facing some type of problem, the first thing to do is to identify exactly what you think that difficulty may be. Define it. You need to know what needs "fixing" before you can actually fix it! So, take as much time as you need, go over the situation, go over your behavior, and, go over the behavior of others, if others were somehow involved.

Also, try to remember what was said and what you thought before, during, and immediately after the situation occurred. Additionally, review where you were at the time that you believe the problem initially arose.

If you are getting our drift, you will see that you must look at everything related to the situation in order to decide exactly what the problem is. Do not get upset if you do not identify the problem correctly, especially at the start of your investigation. It takes some time and practice to learn how to effectively identify a problem.

2. Generate Alternatives

OK. So now you have some idea of what your problem is. Then, the next step is to generate alternatives, or, in other words, come up with some viable courses of action to take in response to the problem. At this step, or, at least, at the beginning of this step, do not censure yourself (within reason, of course). Clear your mind and attempt to generate or come up with as many alternatives as you can.

Then, WRITE THEM DOWN ON PAPER! Get a pad and pen or pencil and write! Do not limit yourself by relying on your memory. You will invariably forget some of the alternatives that you so painstakingly generated if you do not put them down on paper.

So, make yourself comfortable and begin your list. Make a list of the possible courses of action that you think MAY resolve the problem at hand. For your convenience, we have included a Problem Check List form for your use. You will find this form toward the end of the book in Appendix III. Since we would like to help you get started, we have also included some possible alternative behavioral suggestions for your review (same Appendix).

3. Select an Alternative

Assuming that you have identified the problem and have generated enough viable alternatives from which to choose your first course of action, it is now time to select the course of action that you feel confident in taking. By confident, we mean that you feel that this particular course of action will, hopefully, do the trick, so to speak, to resolve your current problem.

With your list in hand, take some time to mull over all of the alternatives that you came up with until you are familiar and comfortable with them. At this point, you should also consider the possible consequences that would accompany each of the respective alternatives. When all of this is done, you would pick one of the alternatives to use. Again, choose the one that you feel will best solve your specific problem in a way that is appropriate and acceptable to yourself (not to mention, society).

4. Act

Are you still with us? Good. At this point in the problem-solving process, you should know what your problem is; you should have your alternatives generated; and, you should have selected the course of action that you THINK will BEST resolve the issue at hand. So, what's next? Obviously, ACT!

After choosing the course of action, act on it. Put the specific alternative to the test by applying it to your particular problem situation. In other words, take the action in an attempt to resolve the issue.

5. Review

Let us assume that you have acted on your chosen course of action. You are now in a
position to take the next step, which is to review the consequences of your selected alternative. In other words, go back and take another look at the original problem. Then, look at the solution chosen and the results of your choice. Following this, ask yourself: "Did my chosen solution really take care of the problem, or, is the problem still present in some form"?

If your answer to the above question is: "Yes, my problem has been dealt with successfully and no longer exists", then you have really got something! You have developed a strategy that has proven itself successful. It works! Great! If this is the case, the net result of your problem-solving efforts is twofold.

First, you now have a technique that you can use when, and if, this type of problem resurfaces at some time in the future. And second, you have also developed a strategy that you can initially try when faced with similar types of problems in the future. Of course, some modifications may have to be made, but, at least you now have a starting point with a proven track record. You are now "miles ahead" of where you were originally!

However, as we have indicated above, this is not a perfect world. So, perhaps, upon your reflection, you find that the solution that you thought would work---did not. Perhaps, upon review, you find that you are still left with the problem or some form thereof. What do you do now? Well, this brings us to our final step, and, that is to return to step #2.

6. Return to Step #2

If, after all of your work, you find that your selected alternative did not work on the existing problem, you will need to return to your list of alternatives, review it, and, after additional careful thought, select a second course of action.

Then, take this second alternative and apply it to the problem. As before, once you have acted, review the results to see where you and your problem now stand. If your second choice turns out to be the "ticket to success", great! If not, then, yes, you've guessed it. Go back to your list once again and select a third course of action, act on it, and, as always, review the results.

However, at this point, if you are on your third "let me try this course of action" on the same problem, then, it probably would not be such a bad idea to go back to your initial statement of the problem to make absolutely sure your UNDERSTANDING/PERCEPTION of the problem is both realistic and accurate. If it is, leave it alone. But, if you determine that your initial interpretation of the problem may have been incorrect, then, rewrite the problem in more realistic and more accurate terms. And then, continue through step #6.

At this time, we think you should have a general idea of how this problem-solving process works. We understand that it may seem like a lot of work, and, at first, it is. But, it is definitely worth it. And, you will more than likely find that, once you establish an arsenal of strategies, you will have developed a "bank account", if you will, from which to draw when future problems arise---and, make no mistake about it, they will arise!

Remember, the problem-solving steps, as outlined above, are always the same and used in the same sequence. It is the problem that changes. And, when the problem changes, the strategies generated may also change to reflect the new problem. Just be patient with yourself. Rome wasn't built in a day and you are not going to solve all of your stress producing problems in a day either.

But, as you become more proficient with your problem-solving skills, you will experience a greater sense of security, less stress, and, perhaps most importantly, be able to deal more easily with your children. As a side note, these steps can also be used for your children's problems or for when your children ARE the problem!

At this juncture, we feel that it would be a good idea to do a brief review of what has transpired thus far in this chapter on stress management. First of all, you learned about eliminating all the "musts", "shoulds", and, "oughts", etc. from your vocabulary. Secondly, you found out that indulging yourself with some periods of "time-out" is a luxury that you can well afford. And finally, we discussed the fine art of problem-solving. Hopefully, you are still with us.

IV. The Fourth Strategy in Managing Your Stress is Closely Related to the Aforementioned Issue of Problem-Solving. This Fourth Strategy Involves Identifying Who Actually Owns the Problem

When something occurs that appears to be problematic, you need to look at the situation and determine who really owns the problem---BEFORE you get deeply involved with it! In other words, you should ask yourself: "Is this problem really mine or does it belong to someone else"?

If the problem DOES NOT belong to you, throw it away. Get rid of it immediately and get on with your own business. You have enough in your life to be concerned about without taking on the problems that rightfully belong to another adult.

However, if you find that the problem IS yours, then it would be wise to go back to the previously outlined six steps for your problem-solving. Go over the steps, and, more importantly, use them. But, just in case this idea of problem-ownership is a bit confusing, permit us to give you an example.

An instance, among many, in which you would not own the problem would be in the case of a dispute between two co-workers or colleagues. This is not your problem so don't make it yours! It is their problem. It is their dispute. So, stay out of it. However, if the dispute is between YOU and a co-worker or colleague, then, unfortunately, the problem IS yours and must be dealt with accordingly.

Fortunately, if you have been reading closely, you now have the techniques at your disposal to, hopefully, be successful in resolving the difficulty and lowering your level of stress. Learning to identify who owns the problem can go a long way to saving you a lot of unnecessary stress, not to mention headaches and sleepless nights. And remember, the less stressed you become, the smarter and more effective you should be with your children.

V. LAST, BUT CERTAINLY NOT LEAST, WHEN TRYING TO REDUCE YOUR STRESS, LEARN TO "PICK YOUR BATTLES"

In today's society, when you deal with other people, you are inevitably going to come across situations which, on the surface, appear to be ripe for a battle and/or argument---especially where your children are concerned. But, you do not have to "bite". When you feel that someone is pushing your argument and/or stress buttons, do not react immediately. Step back and give yourself a chance to think. Is this situation worth a verbal confrontation or not?

If you determine that it is not, then, leave it alone! But, if the situation seems to necessitate some type of DISCUSSION with the aim toward resolution, then you can take the discussion route.

In basic terms, this is the act of choosing your battles. Those of you with children (which are probably all of you)---especially teenagers---know what we mean. Just because someone else is in a confrontational mood, that does not automatically mean that you also have to be in that same frame of mind. Get out while the getting is good.

Just as an aside, two people confronting each other in argumentative terms, generally never solves a thing. So, why take on the added stress? It doesn't make any sense for you and your own peace of mind. In the long run, your parenting efforts and interpersonal relationships will suffer.

Chapter 13

ADOLESCENCE
(HELP!! HELP!! HELP!!)

Now that you have some idea about reducing your stress and giving yourself some relaxation time, we felt that this would be as good a time as any to "attack" that all-important period of life called adolescence. Now, don't let the subject matter, or, more specifically, the age level to be discussed in this chapter, scare you. For the most part, adolescence is really relatively harmless---if it's approached in a smart and appropriate manner.

However, for many people, the topic of adolescence does tend to be met with some trepidation. In fact, for some, the mere idea of their children becoming adolescents scares the h**// out of them. This is especially true if the children in question were somewhat out of control PRIOR TO the advent of their adolescent years.

But, having one or more adolescents in the household needn't be something to fear, nor does it have to be a time of serious trouble and turmoil in the home. Yes, it can easily be problematic. But, serious problems are not inevitable.

Prior to continuing, however, allow us to point out---and correct---a common misconception that many people share about entering, and exiting, this time of life called adolescence.

In years gone by, it was generally believed and accepted that a child became an adolescent at 13 years of age and ceased being an adolescent on his or her 20th birthday. In other words, this thinking held that adolescence encompassed the teenage years---ages 13 through 19, inclusive. However, that idea has changed somewhat in recent years.

Specifically, it is now believed that a child begins his or her entrance into adolescence with puberty. For some, particularly girls, this can be as young as 10 ½ years of age. For others, both boys and girls, the start of puberty can be at a point later than 13 years of age. It is really quite individual. However, in relation to the previous sentence, we feel that a note of caution is probably warranted.

As a parent, it would be wise to consult with your child's pediatrician, on a regular basis, (check-ups for your child, etc.) to help ensure that your child's development is proceeding appropriately, given the child's gender and age. And, if you feel that your child may be entering puberty too early or that your child is somewhat delayed with puberty, you must speak with the pediatrician in a timely manner about this issue and establish a course of action to follow.

Now, at the other end of the adolescent spectrum is the issue of the age at which the child leaves adolescence to become a young adult. If you review a large number of books on this subject, believe it or not, you will find that there are some volumes that report something akin to the following: A person does not leave the adolescent stage of life until he or she has assumed all of the responsibilities of adulthood. While some scholars swear by this idea, we, your humble psychologists, do not.

Consider this: Think about all of the individuals that you know who are in their early-to-mid-twenties and think about what they are doing with their lives. Some may be in college; some may be working part-time or full-time; still others may be doing some combination of these things. However, chances are that many of them are probably still living at home with mother still doing their laundry, still regularly cooking for them, and, still doing their cleaning.

Yet, they can generally come and go as they please and, they can stay at home, alone, for extended periods of time while the parents are away. In addition, they no longer need the type of close supervision one would give to a teenager (we hope!).

Now, when you think about it, individuals matching the aforementioned description, really do not have "all of the responsibilities of adulthood". Yet, would we still call them adolescents? We think not. Some may disagree with us, and that's OK. But, in our professional opinion, these young men and women are no longer in adolescence. So, contrary to some theorists, we believe that by age 20, adolescence is a thing of the past.

Now, where were we before we got ever so slightly off track? (Oh those digressions!) Oh, yes. We were noting that the adolescent years do not have to be too much of a problem for parents. However, please do not get us wrong. We are not saying that the adolescent years will always be a peaceful and pristine time of life for the family. This would not be realistic, especially in today's world.

However, that said, having an adolescent (or 2, or 3 or…!) at home does not have to be all that bad either, despite what you may have read and/or heard. The important thing to keep in mind is that, during these years, the goal for parents is to find that all-important "happy medium", within which the parent and the adolescent can live in relative peace and harmony. While this goal may be difficult for some, perhaps many, families (depending on the adolescent AND the parents), this goal is not impossible.

Related to the above, it is important to also keep in mind that, most of the negative hype that you hear about and read about regarding the population that we know as adolescents, is just that---HYPE! The so-called negative stories are usually reported in a sensational manner and, when all is said and done, sensational stories sell papers and/or make for shocking newscasts. An unfortunate side-effect of all this is that these types of stories tend to give the mistaken impression that seriously problematic adolescents are the norm, rather than the exception.

However, you can rest easy, folks. The truth of the matter is that adolescents with serious problems make up a relatively small percentage of the overall adolescent population. The vast majority of adolescents are respectable, hard-working, caring kids who generally stay out of serious trouble and are not bent on making their parents' lives as miserable as possible!

This is not to say, however, that adolescents do not try their parents' patience. The fact is that ANY child---adolescent, or otherwise---will, from time to time, wear a parent's patience quite thin. This is only normal, and, it is to be expected. So, the trick is that you really need to learn how to smartly handle those instances when you feel your patience wearing thin. And, if you have been following along thus far, you should be aware of the fact that, how you, as the parent, react to your adolescent's misbehavior, has a profound influence on how well your patience---and sanity---will survive your children's adolescence.

Yes, adolescents do have problems. Yes, adolescents will misbehave. Yes, adolescents have difficulty from time to time with their emotions. They can be argumentative. They can be periodically lazy. They can be demanding. They can be_____(you can fill in the blank). But, adolescents do not have a corner on the market when it comes to these and other aspects of their lives.

ALL age groups, from the very youngest to the very oldest, can, and do, have problems. You can take the aforementioned seven sentences and you can substitute just about any other similar term for almost any other age group, and the sentences would continue to be accurate---and, they would also make perfect sense!

What is the point of all this, you may ask? Well, the point is this: Don't lump all adolescents together (or any other age group, for that matter), and, don't treat each one as if he or she were a carbon copy (how's that for an old-fashioned term?) of every other he and she in that age range. Remember, everyone is different, and, everyone needs to be treated as an individual.

Now, if you, the reader, are ready, please allow us to return to a statement that we made a few paragraphs ago. Just to refresh your memory, we noted that, how you, as the parent, reacts to your adolescent's misbehavior, has a profound influence on how well your patience (and sanity) will survive.

As we have alluded to previously in this book, when discussing interactions between parents and their children, whether those children be adolescents or younger, reacting becomes a very important part of the situation in question. Reacting is important because, when parents react, they are merely "bouncing off" of whatever it was that their child said and/or did that was not acceptable. As a result of this "bouncing off", nothing constructive occurs and the scene is now set for an unfortunate chain of reactions to happen.

For example, the child/adolescent does or says something that can be loosely construed as a misbehavior. Then, if the parents react, they usually become quite emotional and reason, sanity, and logic tend to go right out the window. Once the parents' reaction is over, then, almost on cue, it is the child's/adolescent's turn to react to the parents' reaction. And, can you guess what happens next? Of course you can because it is probably happening in your own home---otherwise you wouldn't be reading this book!

So, what happens next? The parents then react to their child's reaction to their own initial reaction! Get the picture?

This type of fruitless interaction will usually continue until one side literally gives up. Unfortunately, it is usually the uninformed (about smart parenting, that is) parents who run out of steam first, and give up. And, when this occurs, the child/adolescent generally perceives himself or herself as the winner in this conflict. Consequently, the parents accomplished absolutely nothing.

In attempting to prevent this type of scenario from occurring, the key is for the parents to ACT rather than REACT. If parents act rather than react, they have a much better chance of remaining in control of their emotional state and, hopefully, maintaining their sanity and reasoning skills.

Granted, it is difficult not to react. And, it is even more difficult for impulsive parents than for those parents who have mastered the fine art of thinking before speaking and/or acting. Yes, acting and not reacting is difficult---but it is not impossible.

Somewhat related to the issue of acting versus reacting, is the concept of "picking your battles", which, as you may recall, we touched upon in the stress management chapter (Chapter 12). One of the most important things for parents to keep in mind when an adolescent occupies one of the bedrooms in the home, is to PICK YOUR BATTLES! This is so important---and often overlooked---that we will repeat it: PICK YOUR BATTLES!

Remember, not everything your adolescent says or does is cause for the eruption of a volcano/battle. As parents of an adolescent, you must learn to let a lot of relatively unimportant things slide---like water off a duck's back.

Now, please do not misunderstand what we are saying. We are not saying that you should ignore most of what your adolescent says or does. Nor are we saying to take whatever your adolescent son or daughter says or does, lightly. This would border on being negligent as a parent. And, as parents, the last thing that you would want is to be negligent.

However, what we ARE saying is to keep a watchful eye, know your adolescent's friends, and, know, to the best of your ability, how your adolescent spends his or her time---both at home and away from home. In short, be good, caring, concerned, involved parents. And, do not fight and argue over every little thing. It's not worth it and it is not necessary. And, when all is said and done, all of this unnecessary bickering is not good for your relationship with your child.

It is never worth it to have a battle over everything---or over almost everything---which is what occurs in more homes than you would imagine. Believe us when we say that this type of battleground exists in many homes where adolescents and their parents try to reside in peaceful, harmonious co-existence.

But, that battleground does not have to be present in YOUR home just because you have a child who happens to be an adolescent. In the long run, it's really up to you.

At this point, you are probably wondering: "How do I just pick my battles? It sure sounds good, but, can it really be done?" Our answer to this query is a resounding YES! We will concede that it is not the easiest thing in the world to do, but, with some patience, perseverance, and practice, this "picking your battles" thing should be able to be accomplished.

At this juncture, we believe that a strong word to the wise is in order. Pay close attention because, if the shoe fits…well, you know the rest. So, follow along and heed the following warning. If you are, what is politely termed, a control freak, picking your battles will probably be somewhat more difficult than it would be for the non-control freak parent.

Consider this. A person who has a strong need to control all that lies within and around his or her environment, will probably be at odds with just about anything his or her adolescent says or does. As a result, the battle lines would have been drawn quite early in the overall scheme of things. That controlling person will, more often than not, be ready for battle at a moment's notice. And, if professional experience serves as any barometer, an adolescent, or, for that matter, any child, doesn't stand a chance with anything, if one or both parents have a thing with super-control.

It really will not matter what the adolescent says or what the adolescent does. The roles of the scene are set. The controlling parent wants his or her way, and, what the adolescent wants is automatically given a "thumbs down". The battle then ensues, and, as is usually the case in these types of circumstances, nobody really wins. Oh, the parent may THINK he or she has won something, but, in the long run, the parents really lose. And, unfortunately, so, too, does the adolescent.

So, as if you haven't guessed by now, one of the first ways of preventing this type of scenario from occurring, and, the first step toward successfully picking your battles, is to get rid of that over-the-top control thing. You, as the parent, must understand that you cannot realistically control everything, least of all every aspect of your adolescent's life.

Now, before you start jumping up and down, hear this. Obviously, there are some circumstances where parental control is needed, if not, essential. These would include, but not be limited to, setting reasonable and appropriate limits for your adolescent to abide by; enforcing appropriate discipline in the home; insisting on good, sound, moral values and behavior; having your adolescent help out at home with chores; setting reasonable curfews; and, not accepting any disrespect from your adolescent.

And, please remember, as we have pointed out above, this is only a very brief sampling of areas where parental control needs to be present. Remember, to be successful in picking your battles, you must establish, early on, when your control, and/or authority, will ultimately prevail without question.

To continue. If you REALLY want success with picking your battles wisely, you need to know what those "I-should-not-pick-a-battle" instances would look like. So, to make it a little easier for you, we have put some "I-should-not-pick-a-battle" examples into a list, a list to which you can refer as often as you would like. Also, we would like to point out that the items on the list are in no particular order of importance. And, just as with the examples of when control is needed, the following list is also not exhaustive.

However, just another word about the items on the list. As the parents, there is no law against you giving your opinion about anything pertaining to your adolescent---or to any of your children, for that matter. But, with the "I-should-not-pick-a-battle" types of situations, once you state your opinion, then, that's it! State your opinion, and then, keep quiet. If you continue with your anti-whatever opinion, the situation will then escalate into a battle. So, be careful!

Since our "I-should-not-pick-a-battle" list, together with our explanations, appears to be a bit lengthy, we decided to move to a new chapter to cover these issues. Wow! Two chapters on adolescents! Our own adolescent---when he was an adolescent, that is---would have been very impressed!

Chapter 14

MORE ADOLESCENCE!

Well, as promised, here's the "I-should-not-pick-a-battle" list.

LIST

1. Hair: Style, color, length, etc.
2. Music (with the exception of violent, vulgar, and sexually explicit lyrics).
3. Neatness, or lack thereof, of your adolescent's room.
4. Clothing (within reason, of course).
5. How the clothing is worn (again, within reason).
6. Getting a driver's license, at the legal age, of course.
7. Most foods eaten (here you have some indirect control if you do the shopping and the cooking).
8. Friends, assuming they are not law breakers.
9. Time to get up in the morning
10. Time to go to bed at night

OK. Now that you have absorbed the aforementioned list, allow us to say a few words (hopefully, only a few words because, as we write these illustrious words, it is almost midnight!) concerning each of the items on the list. And, remember, these are areas in which you, as the parent, really do not have much control.

As we refer back to the list, we see that the first item that we mentioned was hair. In doing so, we intend the category of hair to cover such things as color, length, style, and, last but not least, the voluntary lack thereof (of hair)!

OK, color. As you are probably aware, the average child will generally have brown, black, and, to a lesser extent, blond or red hair. Not to mention, of course, all of the various shades that are contained under the aforementioned overall colors. But, these colors aside, there are quite a few adolescents out there who will "experiment" with, shall we say, somewhat unusual hues of the scalp!

Over the years, we have seen all sorts of tones upon the heads of adolescents. We have seen blue hair, green hair, orange hair, purple hair, lavender hair, and, pink hair, just to name a few. Naturally, to the adult observer, it all looks ridiculous, right? But, to the adolescent with such a glowing mane, he or she is expressing his or her individuality---or, whatever the term is that is currently in vogue.

As a reasonable parent, you probably will not appreciate your adolescent's new crop. In fact, you will, more than likely, hate it! Also, as the parent, you will hope that it will all just go away---the hair color, not the kid! And, if you are true to form, you will probably be trying to figure out which is the lesser of the two evils---letting the unusual color stay, or, looking at a bald adolescent, male or female! You may even have thoughts of shaving your child's head while he or she is sleeping (we wouldn't recommend this!).

But, after reading this far in this book and consistently applying what you have learned, we can hopefully say that that was the "old" you. The you who wanted to control everything. The you who didn't know how to "pick your battles". The you…well, you get the picture!

Actually, when it comes to hair, battle-picking is really quite simple. All you have to do is to keep repeating to yourself---or to whoever will listen---"It can be washed out!", or, "It will grow out---eventually!" Remember, it's you adolescent's hair---not yours! If your child wants to walk around in public being stared at or whispered about because of hair color, well, that's life. If your child gets ridiculed, laughed at, or, worse yet, shunned, because of a hair color, then, so be it. It will be a hard lesson to learn, but, the lesson will not be forgotten anytime soon!

The bottom line here is that this is one battle that you really do not need. So, don't make this nonissue an issue. If you are attempting to make some headway (pardon the pun) at picking your battles, do not make this one of your battles. It is really not that important in the overall scheme of things. When you think about it, there are far worse things that your adolescent could be doing. Hair color is not one of those far worse things!

There is one other item that we would like to touch upon before we leave the wonderful world of hair. Now, we just know that some of you parents out there are probably thinking: "Oh no! We have a wedding, graduation, confirmation, bar mitzvah_____(you can fill it in) to attend! Family will be there!

Aunt (whomever) will be there! Uncle (whomever) will be there! MY MOTHER WILL BE THERE!!! And, our beautiful child has purple and orange hair! What are we going to do? We will "die" of embarrassment!"

Well, our answer to all of this is: No, you will not die of embarrassment because YOU should not be the one being embarrassed. Remember, it's not YOUR hair on top of your adolescent's head. It's your ADOLESCENT'S hair! If anyone is going to be embarrassed, it will be your adolescent---not you! So, keep that in mind!

What this all boils down to is that it is your adolescent's problem, so, don't make it yours (remember, problem ownership?). It is your adolescent's embarrassment, so, don't make it yours.

With that, we will now leave the interesting world of adolescent hair and go on to the next thing on our unprioritized list---music. What can we say? Different generations have different tastes in music. If you go back through the twentieth century, it seems that, during any given decade, the older generation of the time felt that the younger generation's musical tastes were, to put it mildly, nonexistent---and, sometimes, even obscene!

Consider the original rock 'n roll from the 1950's. The kids growing up during that era loved it, but, for the most part, their parents did not. The parents usually complained that no one could understand the lyrics and that the gyrations of the performers were, to say the least, vulgar. Yet, the kids loved it!

When rock 'n roll gave way to the British invasion of the mid-60's, the same thing happened---the kids loved it while the parents complained that the music was too loud and that the long hair on the male performers was shocking! In the 1980's, we saw the dawn of, what we believe was termed, heavy metal. Again, the kids loved it and, as before, the parents (including us!) hated it.

And so it goes, generation after generation. Each generation seems to have some type of problem with the musical tastes of it's children---not 100% across the board, mind you, but still, it's probably close.

So, as a parent, EXPECT that your adolescent will indulge in the music of the day. It's only normal. Your child's music may or may not be to your liking, and, if it is not to your liking, is it really such a problem that it has to become a battle? Of course it isn't!

You will be amazed at how your adolescent's tastes will change as he or she matures. Why, your child may even begin listening to and enjoying the original rock 'n roll, or, even more shockingly, big band swing!

So, the moral of the story is to keep an open mind and do not try to control your adolescent's listening habits. It should all work out without a battle being waged. However, at this point, we sense that a few caveats appear to be in order regarding music.

First of all, let's start with the noise level, which, if not addressed, can be deafening. Adolescents do tend to blast their music (for the sake of argument, we are calling it music!) until your walls vibrate and you can't hear yourself think.

This happens. But, it IS your house, and, as the parents, you are perfectly entitled to establish a noise-level-limit, above which you will not tolerate. And, you need to set that limit early and stick to it!

If the noise level is too much, tell your adolescent to lower the volume. And, while you're at it, explain to your music lover why the volume should be lowered, and together, try to find a volume level that would be acceptable to all concerned. Then, if your adolescent violates the agreed upon limit, then no music, temporarily, until he or she learns to be considerate of the others living in the household. But, as we have noted elsewhere in this book, when instituting consequences, START SMALL!

For example. You can start by prohibiting the playing of music for the remainder of that day. But, remember to let the child know that he or she can resume listening to the music---at the appropriate volume---on the following day. This will give the adolescent a chance to show that cooperation with parents IS possible! If, on the following day the music is again too loud, repeat the above. Repeat the above until your adolescent LEARNS AND FOLLOWS the volume rules.

Of course, you must realize that, when you are not at home, you really have no control over the volume of your adolescent's music playing. So don't get yourself in a tizzy. As with any child and any behavior, you can only hope that there will be some carryover of your limits during the times when you are nowhere in sight.

A second, and perhaps, more important, warning that all parents must heed is to pay attention to the lyrics of the "songs" that your son or daughter may be listening to. Under no circumstances should you allow violent, obscene, sexually explicit, or satanic lyrics to be played by your child in your home---and, if possible, anywhere else! Talk with your adolescent (or any age child, if it applies), explain your reasons as to why these types of lyrics are not acceptable and/or suitable, and then, follow through on the ban.

You may get an argument, and, you probably will. However, do not weaken. It is vitally important to your child's well-being to forbid the types of lyrics mentioned above. If you do get a battle, then, so be it. In other words, this IS one battle to pick, if necessary, to protect your child. After all, protecting your child of any age is, and should be, your utmost goal. Society isn't going to do it, so you must!

Now, getting back to our abbreviated list, we will tackle the issue of neatness in your adolescent's room. While the neatness of a child's room seems to always be high on a parent's list of priorities, in reality, it's really not that important. It would be nice (remember? keep the stress down) if your adolescent's room was neat, or, at least, somewhat neat. But, if it's not, it's not.

Oooh! We can "hear" parents all across book-reading land huffing and puffing on this one! So, as all of you huff and puff, let us clarify what we are referring to when we talk about a lack of neatness in an adolescent's room.

When we refer to a room not being neat, we are talking about things such as clothes being strewn about; books and/or magazines being on the floor; clutter being caused by an overabundance of electrical/audio/video components all over the place; papers covering almost every horizontal surface; etc. We think you get the picture---a messy one, but still, a picture.

However, we are not including food, junk or otherwise, or beverages, in our definition of a messy room. Edible items must be taken out of the room on at least a daily basis. This also includes dirty bowls and dishes, as well as used glasses, cups, cans, etc. In other words, anything related to food, drink, and their respective containers, cannot be left in a child's room to spawn nasty odors and mold, not to mention, bugs!

So, parents, stop huffing and puffing and see to it that the edible items, and their containers, are taken out of your children's rooms. Every other legal thing that you allow your child to have---don't worry about it! Just keep in mind that the room "belongs" to your child. It is his or her little sanctuary of privacy. So, don't make it's physical appearance the source of a battle. It's really not worth it. Just keep the door SHUT!

Moving on, we will next tackle clothing. Let us start off by saying the obvious: As with the music, different generations have different clothing styles. It's that simple! Just think back to when you were a teenager all those years ago (sorry!). Chances are your parents were not too crazy about your mode of dress either. So, settle down and try to roll with the style that is "in vogue" at the prevailing moment in your teenager's life. Needless to say, common sense, good judgment, and a sense of decency must prevail regardless of what your adolescent wants to wear.

When you consider the range of clothing that is available at any given point in time, you can see that there are certainly various types of styles that are simply not appropriate for teenagers to wear. And, just as with the volume of music, it is up to the parents to set the limits. For example, tight clothing, revealing clothing, and clothing that looks like it should be on a thirty-year-old rather than on a 15 year old, should be off limits.

You are the parents, you set the rules. We believe that, if you are reasonably fair and reasonably objective, you should not experience any serious clothing battles in your home. And, a good relationship with your adolescent can only serve to help your cause. Again, as mentioned above, have an honest and loving talk with your child about his or her clothing and about your concerns. Then, stick to your guns!

In a related vein, our #5 item, how the clothing is worn, is also not a battle you want to pick. Again, good judgment, a sense of decency, common sense, and good reason will go a long way to keeping everyone concerned satisfied. Obviously, if the clothing is dirty, or cutting off the adolescent's circulation, or loose enough to fall off of his or her body, it should not be worn.

But, do not go overboard with this issue. Realize that times have changed since you were a teenager, and, consequently, as we have said, styles have followed suit. However, if you keep the aforementioned aspects of good judgment and common sense, etc., in mind, together with a good relationship with your adolescent, this area should remain a non-issue. And, dressed appropriately, your older adolescent should look very good behind the wheel of the car. How's that for a "shift" (pardon the pun) in issues!

Driving...It's every parent's "dream"---and, every parent's "nightmare", and, as you may recall, it is the sixth item on our list. To be more specific, it is a dream because the time has come when most, if not all of the chaufferring for this child is finally behind you. But, it is also a nightmare because of the dangers involved with driving. Even if your adolescent turns out to be (and we hope he or she does) one of the safest drivers the world has ever seen, a caring parent will still remain very much concerned because there are so many other drivers to be concerned about. And, therein lies the problem.

Let's face it. Not every driver is a good, safe driver. You don't need us to tell you that drivers' safety records run the gamut from excellent to just plain lousy! But, there are some things that parents can insist on to at least allay some of their fears.

One is to insist that your prospective new driver take a defensive driving course. This type of course should be taken by all drivers, but, since we are talking about adolescents, we'll be consistent and refer only to adolescents. As you may know, these courses are given quite frequently in many locations across the country. And, in addition to the safety concerns, taking one of these courses can, in many states, reduce your insurance premiums. A nice touch!

A second good idea (at least in our professional opinion) is to have a professional and reputable driving instructor teach your teenager how to drive. Most, if not all high schools offer driver training classes for eligible students. It will probably cost a little extra money for the driver training, but, when you consider all of the tension, stress, and headaches that you will avoid by not being your child's teacher, you will soon see that it will be money well spent.

If you, as the parents, insist on at least these two things AND enforce your rules for car usage (again, after a heart-to-heart talk), then, the issue of driving should not become a battle to be picked. Bear in mind, however, that, if your child becomes reckless and/or careless behind the wheel, then your child's driving will---and should---become an issue. The bottom line is this: No teenager (nor anyone else, for that matter) should be driving who is reckless, careless, and irresponsible. Likewise, no teenager (nor anyone else) should be driving who is under the influence of alcohol, drugs, or some combination thereof.

Moving on, the seventh item on our "I-should-not-pick-a-battle" list concerns your teenager's eating practices. As we stated previously, you DO have some control in this area if you, the parent, are the one who does the grocery shopping and the cooking. And, as in most households, it IS the parent who attends to the aforementioned tasks---not the teenager.

But, when discussing eating behavior, you must remember that, once your child leaves the house, you no longer have any control over what he or she eats. Just accept that! Let it go! You'll feel much better.

All you can do in this realm is to provide nourishing meals for your child to eat when he or she is dining at home. In addition, you can also discuss with your child your views on what would be acceptable foods to eat when that child is eating away from your abode. Then, hope for the best!

The bottom line here is this: Provide good nutritious meals at home, and, hope that you have instilled enough sensibility in your adolescent that he or she will usually---not always---select foods that would meet with your approval and maintain his or her good health.

Hopefully, you have digested (again, pardon the pun) what we have been discussing thus far. If not, there is always time for a little re-reading. But, whether digested or not, we must continue with our eighth item from our list. So, at this point, we are going to take a few moments (or lines) to discuss friends.

It would generally be safe to assume that your adolescent probably knows the types of people that he or she likes as well as the types of peers that he or she doesn't care for for whatever reason. Your adolescent also probably knows the types of individuas that he or she would include in a peer relationship and/or group. However, personality types that your adolescent wishes to spend his or her time with may, and, many times, do, vary drastically from the personality types that you, as the parent, would favor.

Now, as with most everything else, if your adolescent has good common sense and good judgment, not to mention a loving and supportive home and a strong sense of self, then the friends chosen SHOULD be acceptable to you--- not necessarily your "cup of tea"---but, at least, acceptable.

Of course, as the parent, you are perfectly within your rights to CALMLY express your feelings and/or concerns about friend "A" or friend "B". Then--- DROP IT! You really cannot control who your child spends time with once he or she leaves the house on any given day. And remember, the more you talk against someone, the more determined your adolescent usually becomes in "hanging around" with that other person or persons.

So, once your opinion has been stated, watch closely from the sidelines just in case trouble develops. And, if trouble does develop or begins to develop, then, as a concerned parent, you must step in to protect your adolescent from himself or herself.

At this point, we feel that some clarification may be in order. When we speak about friends that do not happen to be your particular "cup to tea", we are referring to relatively decent, average kids who, for one reason or another, you just plain do not take to, so to speak.. Listen, folks, it happens!!

We ARE NOT talking about delinquents, counter-culture types, or adolescents whose behavior borders on the illegal. No, these types are not being included under our umbrella of desirable friends.

Obviously, if your adolescent is thinking of striking up a friendship with one of these types of individuals, then you, again as the caring, concerned parent, must take the steps necessary to try to keep your adolescent from making a terrible mistake. However, rest assured that the delinquent and counter-culture types make up a very small percentage of the overall adolescent population.

Hence, the chances of your average, law-abiding adolescent choosing one of these types of individuals for a "friend", is probably quite small. But, as the parent, you MUST be alert to possible trouble! So, keep your eyes and ears OPEN!!

Now, moving down our illustrious list, you will see that we will next tackle getting up on time in the morning (#9). Needless to say, many adolescents really do not enjoy getting up early in the morning. We think that most "try to" arise very early in the morning because they have to, usually to go to school.

However, please don't misunderstand us. Getting up in the morning is a very good thing. Obviously! It's the "early" part of the equation that usually proves to be a problem. And, please keep in mind that we are referring to the average adolescent in our discussion---not an adolescent who may have a sleep-related disorder. If, by chance, the child does seem to have a sleep-related disorder, then, a medical professional should be consulted immediately.

As many parents know, younger, pre-adolescent children can usually get themselves up at the crack of dawn. However, the same cannot be said for the adolescent. In fact, quite the opposite usually occurs. In other words, it is generally quite difficult for adolescents to wake up very early in the morning ON THEIR OWN! In fact, it is believed that the average adolescent actually needs 10 to 10 1/2 hours of sleep each night in order to function at an optimal performance level.

And, dare we say that most, if not all, adolescents do not get that amount of sleep each and every night. In fact, if you have an adolescent, we think you'll agree that most probably don't even get the usual 8 hours of sleep each night---so, forget about 10 to 101/2!

When you examine a typical adolescent's schedule (yes, many ARE typical), it becomes quite clear why getting a good night's sleep may not---or, cannot---be a top priority. Think about it. You have the adolescent usually starting school each day somewhere between 7:30 a.m. and 8:00 a.m., which, by necessity, means that many must be up and ready to catch the school bus by 6:30 a.m. or 7:00 a.m.---sometimes, even earlier! And, if the adolescent is involved with some school-related extracurricular activity, such as band, that practices BEFORE the school day begins, the aforementioned times would be adjusted accordingly.

In addition, many teenagers participate in after-school extracurricular activities, such as sports. Still others may have a part-time job for after school hours. As a result, the adolescent does not arrive home until almost evening, if not later. Added to this mix, you have dinner and homework, not to mention a social life. All of this takes TIME!

It is no wonder that many adolescents do not get to sleep until very late at night, or in the wee hours of the morning. When this occurs, obviously they are not getting enough hours of sleep, and, consequently, they have a very difficult time getting up early in the morning.

Now, as you are reading this, you are probably wondering what all this has to do with picking your battles. Well, it's really quite simple, we think. YOU cannot get up for your adolescent. Your adolescent has to get up for himself or herself. So, you need to calmly discuss the situation with your teenager, express your feelings and concerns, and, TOGETHER, brainstorm some solutions (see "problem-solving") that would lead to the adolescent getting up when he or she must get up.

One possible solution would be to buy a clock with a very loud and long-lasting alarm. Your teenager can also place the clock across the room from his or her bed, thus necessitating that he or she would have to get his or her body out of bed in order to shut off the annoying alarm. Another option can be to go over your adolescent's schedule---again, working together---to see where modifications can be made (remember the Activity-Time Chart?). And then, make them!

In case you haven't guessed, these suggestions can be used together as part of a comprehensive plan that may enable your adolescent to get up in the morning by virtue of his or her "own steam", if you will.

However, please keep in mind that, if whatever you try does not work and your adolescent still will not get up in a timely manner, then, he or she must face the consequences AT SCHOOL for being late to school. Yelling, screaming, and banging on your child's bedroom door every morning, will not do the trick. Some careful planning, along with the appropriate consequences, should. But, the situation should not be a battle! So, don't pick one!

As we are making our way down our list, we have finally come to the last, but certainly not the least, item. Just to refresh your memory (and to save you the trouble of turning back the pages) that last item, which is directly related to the previous one, deals with going to bed---your adolescent, not you!

Again, as with other things on the list, you really cannot force your adolescent to get to bed at any particular time. It just cannot be done! However, if you are that rare parent whose adolescent does have the habit of going to bed, and getting to sleep, at an appropriate time almost every night---all the more power to you! But, you still might want to continue reading this section---just in case. Besides, it's pretty good reading!

To continue. Please keep in mind that, just because your child is in bed at a certain hour, that is no guarantee that he or she will actually go to sleep at that hour. As you may or may not be aware, your adolescent may spend long periods of time, awake, in his or her room---AFTER retiring for the night.

So, what can you, as the parent, do, you ask? Well, since, for our purposes here, the main objective for getting your child to sleep in a timely manner is to try to ensure that he or she will get up on time the next morning, the previous section on getting up would definitely apply in this instance also. Keep in mind that, as long as your adolescent IS getting up in the morning when he or she is supposed to get up, then, getting the adolescent to bed the previous night becomes a non-issue. So, don't make a battle out of bedtime.

However, if your adolescent does not get up in a timely manner, given his or her responsibilities, then some thoughtful problem-solving about getting to bed appears to be in order. And, consider this, if your adolescent is tired during the day simply because he or she WOULD NOT go to bed at an appropriate hour, then, just maybe your adolescent will soon come to the conclusion that getting to sleep at a relatively decent hour may not be such a bad idea after all. Gee…Maybe mom and dad ARE right! Surprise! Surprise!

Well, by this point in our journey, we do hope that you have grasped the concept of "picking your battles", especially when adolescents are involved. Once you master the fine art of differentiating when you should put your two cents in, so to speak, and when you should back off, life with your adolescent should flow a little more smoothly.

Obviously, it will not be perfect---nothing is. But, the stress level in your household should become more manageable. And, when this happens, you and your adolescent can actually enjoy each other's company!

Also, as a reminder, do not forget to provide the warmth, discipline, direction, and support for your adolescent. And, remember to remain an active presence in your adolescent's life. These ingredients are essential for having the best shot at keeping your adolescent "on the right track"---and out of trouble.

In addition, please remember that you are no longer dealing with your young child. You are now dealing with an adolescent who is an emerging young adult. Consequently, your interactions must be altered to a certain extent to accommodate this fact of life. Also, be alert, be aware, and, as mentioned above, stay involved in your adolescent's life. It is of utmost importance!

OK. At this point we considered ending our specific focus on adolescents, and hence, ending the current chapter. But, as in most things we do, we usually have just a little more to say (or write? We'll get it right yet!). There is one more point that we would like to make---a point that is focused---hold your breath!--- more on YOU, as the parent, rather than on your adolescent, per se.

So, if you follow along, in a non-defensive manner, of course, and, if what we are about to say sounds somewhat familiar, then, you may need to take some type of action to remedy the situation. If action is needed (perhaps talking to an appropriate professional), and you take that appropriate action, then, by helping yourself, you should indirectly influence---and, hopefully, enhance---your relationship with your adolescent, not to mention with any other individuals---children or otherwise---who may be living in your household.

At this time, do we "hear" you wondering what it is that we are referring to? Well, to put it as succinctly as possible (before we elaborate, of course), we are talking about the issue of YOUR mid-life crisis! Now, before you start jumping all over the place yelling: "What the heck does MY mid-life crisis--- if, in fact, I am having one---have to do with my relationship with my teenager", hold your skepticism at bay, stop yelling, start relaxing, and, we will "fill in the blanks" for you.

OK...Are you ready? Well, here it goes......

Oops! Let's not jump the gun! Sorry, folks, but, you'll have to continue holding your skepticism at bay and ceasing your yelling, etc., for just a few more lines (or paragraphs, or pages, depending on how much we write). Upon careful thought, we decided that, the best way to approach this issue was to begin by explaining exactly what a mid-life crisis is. Or, more specifically, outlining what a mid-life crisis may look like to the average person who may be at this stage of life---that dreaded middle-age!

As anyone in middle-age can attest (and, in case you are wondering, we are not admitting anything!), this part of life tends to creep up almost secretly, and, unfortunately, seemingly quite rapidly. And, once it hits, it usually does so with expected, and some unexpected, ramifications. And, those ramifications will most probably be felt not only by the middle-aged person, but also, by anyone who happens to cross the middle-aged person's path!

To begin with, the current thinking has middle-age beginning somewhere between 40 and 45 years of age---some say 40 while others say 45. Take your pick. Either way, it will be here sooner or later. Whichever you choose, middle-age tends to bring on an introspective look into one's current and past life. The person will generally return to the goals made as a young adult and decide whether or not those goals have been accomplished, or, at the very least, were on their way to being accomplished.

Those goals may reflect interpersonal relationships, marital and otherwise; career choice; success as a parent; or, learning some type of skill or sport, etc. Many times a person may review his or her financial situation or health status. And, it is at mid-life that many people first begin to reflect on their own mortality!

Now, if, upon review, the person comes to the conclusion that the important goals and dreams have, in one way or another, been accomplished, then this would be a wonderful thing! However, the problem arises when the person comes to the conclusion that those earlier hopes and dreams, while still somewhat important, were neither met nor were anywhere near being met. In fact, the person may conclude that, now being middle-aged with responsibilities, it may now be "too late" to accomplish what he or she originally set out to do.

One may also realize that life may be almost half over (or, depending on the person, is about half over); that he or she is not as physically strong as in younger days; and, that he or she may not be as healthy as he or she was just 10 years earlier. The person may become more winded more quickly and flights of steps may be feeling just a little bit longer than they used to feel. And, compared to younger ages, running may be slowing to a trot and late nights are becoming earlier and earlier.

We think you get the picture. Life is changing, and, for many people, they tend to not initially view the changes in a positive light. But, please do not misunderstand us here. There are A LOT of positives about being in middle-age. Just being alive immediately comes to mind! However, as human beings, when being introspective in middle-age, we do, for the most part, tend to focus on the negatives and ignore all---or most---of the positives.

So, where does this negative focus leave the average, middle-aged parent? Well, to answer this question, the average, middle-aged parent will probably find himself or herself in a negative state of mind, which, in turn, can lead to some form of depression.

Following from this, with the aforementioned depression, we usually also see an irritable mood, some anxiety, agitation, a general feeling of being "down in the dumps", some appetite disturbance, or problems with concentration and focusing, among other things (as with all of our lists, this list is by no means exhaustive since this book is not about depression).

However, please note: If you are experiencing any of the abovementioned symptoms, and possibly others, it would be wise to speak with your doctor, or with a licensed psychologist and/or psychiatrist, to determine if a true problem does, in fact, exist. Also note that not every middle-aged person will experience age-related emotional difficulties. Some do while others do not. Only YOU can best determine how and what you are feeling.

OK. Now that you have a general idea of what a mid-life crisis looks like, let us get back to the connection between middle-age and adolescence.

Given the ages at which many people start their families, we think it safe to say that many parents are usually advancing through middle-age simultaneously with one or more of their children progressing through adolescence. As a result, you have one or both parents struggling with the aforementioned "symptoms" of a midlife crisis, while, at the same time, you have one or more adolescents rapidly growing and changing, wanting more and more independence and developing ideas, beliefs, and views that do not necessarily agree with their parents' ideas, beliefs, and views.

Consequently, almost before your eyes, the atmosphere in the home can, and often does, become somewhat difficult and volatile. Not only does the adolescent not understand what the parents are going through (nor should they be expected to), but the parents usually do not understand what they themselves are going through! Needless to say, this does make for some interesting interactions---to say the least!

If you read back a few lines (or paragraphs?), you will become aware of one of the solutions to this situation---get professional help, if necessary. As we previously mentioned, if you, as the parent, are experiencing any of the aforementioned feelings and emotions, among others, it would be incumbent upon you to see a qualified professional to sort things out. This way, you can develop a better understanding of the dynamics that may be in play within yourself. The net result should be a better and more understanding relationship between you and your adolescent.

Well, we finally got through adolescence---the chapter, not our ages! And remember, as we had said at the start of this chapter, adolescence is a relatively unique period, when compared to other ages in the life-span. However, we do hope that, after reading these two chapters of the book, you, too, can appreciate the fact that, as parents, you must be objective, fair, and flexible enough to adjust to---and "roll with"---the changes that will inevitably occur as your child goes through his or her teen years. Needless to say, if you are not willing to at least try to be objective, fair, and flexible, we believe that you are, to put it bluntly, asking for unnecessary trouble.

Keep in mind that, as your son or daughter is rapidly moving toward adulthood, your interactions must also change. It will be important to remember that you are no longer dealing with a four-year-old, a five-year-old, a nine-year-old, or, a ten-year-old. You are dealing with someone approaching young adulthood---at least in the latter teen years.

So, change your mindset! If you do, you will, more than likely, reap the rewards and wonder what all the adolescent fuss was about!

However, one more word of caution appears warranted here before we leave this world adolescence. By being objective, fair, and, flexible, and having a changed mindset, DOES NOT MEAN that you have to accept/permit/allow questionable behavior that you previously did not accept/permit/allow. You must use good judgment and common sense. If the behavior doesn't sound and/or "feel" good or acceptable, then, it probably isn't good or acceptable.

Right and wrong does not change with the weather. Your good values and moral beliefs should not change because your child is growing up and may want some of your good values and moral beliefs to change. If they are good, sound values and beliefs, do not allow yourself to be talked into changing them!

Chapter 15

ASK THE PSYCHOLOGISTS

A s we move toward the end of this book, we thought it would be helpful for you to read about some of the concerns that average parents have posed regarding issues related to their children. Along with those questions, we have also included our specific responses that addressed the respective problem situations.

We would also like to refer you back to chapter 1, wherein we listed several types of difficulties that parents might face, at one time or another, with their children. As you read through the following pages, you will see the aforementioned questions being addressed. We do hope that this information will be additionally helpful in your quest toward smart and effective parenting.

Incidentally, many of these questions have been culled from questions received from our numerous television and radio appearances. In addition, the names of the parents have been eliminated from this discourse and the names of the children have been changed.   For ease of reading, we have taken the liberty of leaving the questions and answers in letter form.

So, let us proceed.

Dear Doctor: I am having a problem with my eight year old son, "James". He has always been an average student but was never a behavior problem. However, about two months ago, all of that changed. His grades have been dropping, especially in math, and his teacher has told me that my son has become somewhat of a behavior problem. Needless to say, I was stunned! I'm at my wits end. James tells me that everything is OK, but, after speaking with his teacher, I know that everything is not OK. I would be most grateful for any help with this problem situation.

Dear Parent: You do not say if your son has also begun to misbehave at home. So, we will assume that he has not. Consequently, we need to look at the school situation as the possible source of his problem. What you have described would lead us to suspect that James may be experiencing some type of learning difficulty in the area of mathematics, which, up to this time, has gone unnoticed. It is also possible that, up until about two months ago, he had successfully compensated for whatever learning problem he may have.

Generally speaking, when learning problems go undetected for a period of time, the difficulties tend to begin expressing themselves through some form of misbehavior. This tends to occur, of course, when the compensatory methods that the child had been using, cease to work.

It is interesting to note that his behavior problems coincided with the decline in his academic performance. We would strongly suggest that you speak to the teacher and/or the school psychologist immediately to request a psychological evaluation for your son. This will help to determine if a true learning problem does, in fact, exist.

If a learning problem is present, then the results of the evaluation can guide the professionals at the school on a course of action for your child---a course of action aimed at improving his learning. And, once his alleged learning problem is successfully addressed, any behavioral problems that have appeared, may also lessen, if not disappear.   But, be prepared.   Some counseling may also be necessary to address any residual behavior problems, as well as any remaining difficulties with his self-concept, self-esteem, and, self-confidence.

Dear Doctor: I know this may sound terrible but I simply cannot put up with my child's temper any longer! "Mary" is five years old and she has been having temper tantrums for the past two years. No matter where we are, she screams at the top of her lungs if I dare to tell her "no". We could be in a department store, a supermarket, in our yard, or even in church! If I tell her she can't have or do something, she screams and screams until I eventually give in. In my heart I know that I should not be giving in. But, I can't seem to help it. What can I do before I lose my mind!

Dear Parent: Many children have temper tantrums from time to time, and usually, it is a bid for the parent's attention. It is also a controlling technique that some children quickly learn to use. The only way you are going to stop the tantrums is to change how YOU behave, and/or react, when your daughter goes into her performance. You must learn to stop reacting and to start acting.

In your particular case, this means that you must stop giving in to her unreasonable demands. It also means to NOT give her whatever it is she is looking for, whether this be attention, or some object, or both.

In the space of this letter, it would be impossible to review all of the possible alternatives you could use in your attempts at changing Mary's misbehavior. However, one simple thing you can try is to ignore the temper outbursts. When one starts to ignore tantrums, you must first make sure that your daughter is physically safe, then, leave the room. This should be done in a business-like fashion without any outward expression of emotion attached to your own newly adopted actions.

Needless to say, you must go to a part of the house where you still will be able to keep an eye on Mary, without giving the impression that you are continuing to pay attention to her behavior. We would also suggest that you find a parent education program in your neighborhood to learn other ways to maintain control in your household. Your local school district would be a good place to begin your search for a program. Good luck!

> Dear Doctor: We are having a problem with our eight year old son, "Bobby". He can't seem to make friends. In fact, when I think about it, he never really mingled well with his peers. Most, if not all of his time is spent alone, either watching television, playing games on the computer, or just playing with his toys.
>
> His teacher recently told us that she thinks Bobby is very shy because he does not interact with the other children in the classroom. She did say, however, that he is not a behavior problem and that his grades are "pretty good". Regardless of his good behavior or good grades, my wife and I would like to see our son more socially interactive. What can we do?

Dear Parents of Loner: While your son does not pose any significant behavior or academic problems, we believe that you are justified in being concerned about his lack of interpersonal relationships with his peers. In general, children need to interact with peers, as well as with adults, for the development of good, sound social skills. This social component of a child's life is just as important as the intellectual and physical components, and all must be cultivated and nurtured for optimal development.

As far as helping your son is concerned, you can engage him in one of his favorite games or activities, and, while together, gradually bring up this issue of friendships in order to get his perspective on the situation. Find out if there is a child, or several children, with whom he would like to play. Then, if acceptable, make arrangements for one or more of those children to come to your home to play with your son.

If things work out, one or more of the children can continue to visit your home to socialize with your son. You could also take a small number of them, perhaps one or two, on an outing with your son, going to an appropriate movie, or to a ballgame, etc.

Where school is concerned, you may be able to assist Bobby's teacher in developing ways to motivate him into wanting to participate in small group projects in class. When he does actively participate, his teacher could vigorously reinforce his efforts. Also, speak with the school psychologist about this issue. Perhaps the psychologist can work with your son, either alone or in a small group, to develop new social skills and to enhance them.

Based on the information that you supplied, there is also the possibility that your son may be experiencing some degree of depression. As such, you may want to consider having the school psychologist, or, if you prefer, another licensed psychologist not affiliated with the school, formally evaluate your son to determine if some depression, or some other emotional difficulty, does, in fact, exist.

Taking ALL of these steps would probably be most beneficial for Bobby's optimal growth and development.

Dear Doctor: I would like to ask for some guidance concerning my nine year old daughter, "Penny", who is now in the fourth grade. Prior to this school year, Penny's grades had been fine. However, this year, her grades have only been "so-so", and, they are getting worse. I'm no professional educator, but, I think the problem is that she just hates to read. Over the past 8 or 9 months, I've noticed that she never seems to have a book in her hand. Also, she no longer asks me to buy her books or to take her to the library, as she did when she was younger.

I'm sure her lack of reading is having a detrimental effect on her school performance. I'm puzzled because, a year or so ago, I felt she was very interested in reading, both for school and for leisure. Now, I'm not so sure. Is there anything I can do to try to reverse this unfortunate trend?

Dear Parent of Non-Reader: Since reading is so important as the basis for much of what we learn, you are right to be concerned about Penny's apparent lack of interest in reading. In your letter, you mentioned that her grades this year have been "so-so", which would lead us to assume that, prior to this year, her school performance was acceptable. It would probably be a good idea to discuss this situation with Penny's teacher to get his or her views on what might be going on.

Even though you may have thought your daughter was a good reader in the past, it is quite possible that she may not have been as good a reader as you thought. However, up to the recent past, Penny may have been able to successfully compensate for what may turn out to be a possible reading problem. But now, as she is getting older and her grade level is progressing, required reading is getting more varied and complex, thus rendering her compensatory attempts almost fruitless.

In this type of scenario, it is easy to see how a child can become frustrated with reading and lose interest in it. Obviously, there would be a negative effect on her grades, not to mention her self-concept and self-confidence. In your discussion with her teacher, you may want to request a psychological evaluation to determine if a true reading and/or learning problem does exist. If a problem does exist, then steps can be taken to remediate the situation.

In the meantime, try to rekindle your daughter's interest in reading by putting some high-interest, age-appropriate books around the house in places where you know your daughter will see them. You can also keep several books in the car to encourage reading while traveling. If Penny has an interest in any age-appropriate magazines, you can subscribe to one or more of them. Also, if she is interested in a specific activity, such as dancing, music, or drawing, you can get easy-to-read books on those subjects, read the books with her, and encourage her to talk about what she is reading.

However, please keep this in mind. Do not push her to read just to "see" her reading. You want the resumption of her reading activity to be as natural as possible. But, as we have stated above, talk to her teacher and the psychologist, have some testing done, and, if a true problem exists, have it remediated immediately.

Dear Doctor: My seven year old daughter is in the second grade. Every year, since preschool, the children in her class have handed out Valentine's Day cards to each other. In the past, I would buy my daughter enough cards so that "Mary" would be able to give a card to each and every child in her class.

However, this year, she is being more selective and wants to give cards to only about half of the class. I'm not so sure I like this idea. In my opinion, if a card is not given to every child in the class, then the cards should be mailed. What do you think?

Dear Valentine Mom: We tend to agree with you. We think the practice of handing out Valentine's Day cards in class is inherent with potential problems. We're not saying that problems are inevitable, but, why ask for trouble? For example, there is no guarantee that every child will get a card. So, for those who do not receive a card, there will, more than likely, be hurt feelings along with self-image and self-esteem damage. We liken it to the child who always gets picked last to be in a group or on a class team because no one "wants" him or her to be in their group or on their team.

Related to this, you may have a small number of children in the class who will receive only a handful of cards, as opposed to none, with many more probably getting cards from many classmates. This, too, can have negative effects on self-esteem, self-image, and the feelings of the children.

So, in our professional opinion, unless all of the children in the class are going to receive a lot of Valentine's Day cards, we say, mail them!

Dear Doctor: I am concerned about my teenage daughter. "Alice" is 15 years of age and she appears to be quite popular. She has a lot of friends, she does well in school, and, she has what I consider to be an outgoing personality. You are probably wondering what the problem is. Well, the problem is with OUR relationship.

In the not-too-distant past, we were as close as a mother and daughter could be. At least, I thought we were. We would shop together and have long talks. She would also accompany me on visits to relatives and she seemed to enjoy being at home in the evenings with the family, usually watching television or playing games.

But, over this past year, all of that has changed. She spends so much more time in her room, alone as well as with friends, and a lot less time with me and the rest of the family. Alice is my oldest child and my only teenager. So, I do not have a clue as to how to deal with adolescents. Do you think there is a serious problem here or, am I overreacting? I await your reply.

Dear Alice's Mother: While it is normal and natural for you to be concerned about your daughter's changing behavior, nothing in your letter would lead us to believe that Alice's behavior is abnormal.

Most preadolescent children, by nature and necessity, generally spend a significant amount of time with family, involving themselves in family activities, and, visiting relatives. However, as children pass into adolescence, they tend to seek out increasingly independent lives. This is the time when they begin to separate themselves from family and gravitate more toward peers.

Within the adolescent's circle of friends, you will notice that they talk alike, dress alike, enjoy the same type of music, and sometimes, even wear their hair in the same or similar style. As part of the process of growing up and becoming more independent, adolescents also tend to spend more time "isolated" in their rooms and less time mingling with their parents and siblings.

Your job, as the parent, is to be flexible enough to adjust to these changes taking place within your family. Unfortunately, this is not an easy thing to do. Keeping the lines of communication open will help a great deal. Letting your daughter know that you are there for her when she needs you to be, will also be beneficial.

Of course, as the parent, you must continue to monitor your daughter's behavior and remain an active presence in her life, as you would with any child, being alert to any significant negative changes that might occur. Some changes to look for would include, but are not limited to, a sudden drop in academic performance/grades; an abrupt change in friends; changes in personality; and, a significant degree of seclusion from others.

Consequently, to answer your initial question, based on the information you supplied, it does appear that you are somewhat overreacting at this time. However, please keep in mind that, ANY significant change in a child's personality and/or behavior, should warrant an immediate psychological and/or psychiatric consultation to determine if a significant problem does exist.

Dear Doctor: I have come across something that concerns me but I don't know what, if anything, I should do about it. So, I'm asking you for some ideas. Here's the situation. Over the past several weeks, I have noticed that my neighbor's ten year old son has been walking around the street, alone, at eight or nine o'clock at night. In the mornings, I see him at the school bus stop dressed in light-weight clothing, regardless of the weather conditions. I have also seen an occasional bruise on the child's arm. To make matters worse, this child treats the other young children on the block quite shabbily, so much so that I will not allow my son to play with him.

As far as I know, the boy's mother is a single parent with two older children and one baby. I've thought about talking to the mother, but, I'm not sure that this would be the appropriate thing to do. I just don't know what to do but I know something must be done.

Dear Concerned Neighbor: You are absolutely right! Something definitely needs to be done, and it must be done now! Too much time has already passed. Based on what you describe, a telephone call to the Department of Child Protective Services in your city/county/state should be made for the protection of that child. The telephone number would be listed in your telephone directory. If you cannot find the number, ask your child's teacher or your child's pediatrician. Do not hesitate. A child's well-being is at stake. And remember, one call may not be enough. You need to continue calling until you see that something is being done.

Now, while you let the professionals do their work, you can also do something. You can do the neighborly thing and extend a helping hand to that little boy's mother. She may be just so overwhelmed with the responsibilities of life, in general, and motherhood, in particular. You may want to enlist the help of another mother on your block, and, together, offer some solace for her. It can be something as simple as taking turns looking after her children from time to time to give her a much-needed break.

We realize from your letter that this boy may not be the easiest child to deal with. However, he should not be punished through exclusion for what his mother may or may not be doing. However, at this point, we would not recommend that this child be left alone with other young children, to play or to do otherwise. Perhaps some closely supervised activities would be the order of the day at this time.

In addition, please keep in mind that your neighbor may slam the door in your face and tell you to mind your own business. But, at least you would have tried to do something for that child, and ultimately, for that family.

But, regardless of the outcome of your visit to this mother, that call to Child Protective Services needs to be made immediately!

Dear Doctor: I am the parent of a ten-year-old boy. He is bright, friendly, energetic, and involved in many activities outside the home. Aside from school and homework, his typical week also involves soccer practice, piano lessons, art class, gymnastics, playing with his friends, and so on. It seems as if I am always driving him to one activity or another.

So far, his grades in school have been very good and there have been no complaints from his teacher. However, now he is asking to join a weekly bowling league in addition to everything else he does. How many extracurricular activities can a child of his age successfully manage? Where should I draw the line?

Dear Mother of Busy Child: Over-scheduling children seems to be a common practice in today's society. However, to answer your question, the average ten-year-old child should be able to successfully handle only two or three extracurricular activities. But, as the parent, it is important for you to remember that a child's first, and most important priority, is to do his or her best in school.

Good grades and academic success should not be second to participation in sports, music, and the like. School must come first! Consequently, it is important for you to keep a close watch on your son's academic performance. And, if his grades begin to decline, without the presence of any type of significant learning problem, then it is time to curtail his non-school- related activities.

Another point to keep in mind is that children need some unscheduled free time to play with their friends, to relax, or to just fool around (within reason, of course). In addition, children need time to be with their parents for some family activities.

If you find it necessary to curtail some of your child's activities, have a talk with him and prioritize the importance of each activity. Then, once prioritized, you and your son can begin eliminating what realistically needs to be eliminated.

Drawing the line on outside activities is a tough call for parents to make. But, keeping what we have said in mind, you, as the adult, are the one who must decide when enough is enough. Your son may object to your decision, but, for his own best interests, you need to stand your ground on this issue. Good luck!

Dear Doctor: I am having a problem at home with my three children. And, I desperately need some help! I have three sons, ages four, six, and seven. As you can tell, they are very close in age, which, I think, may be part of the problem. When the three of them are at home, they usually want to play with each other, which, I guess, is a good thing in and of itself.

And, this would normally be fine, except for one thing. When they are playing together, they generally end up arguing about something that one or the other did or did not do. Needless to say, I have to go into the room where they are "playing" to end whatever it is that is going on.

Just like almost any other parent with several children, I would like to see my boys playing nicely without any arguing. This does happen on occasion, but, it is the exception, certainly not the rule. How can I get them to always play nicely?

Dear Mother of Three: Siblings are not going to play quietly every time they get together. There are going to be disagreements. There are going to be some arguments arising. Keep in mind that no child is going to be 100% happy with what another child says and/or does---siblings included. It is just a fact of family life and parents need to get used to hearing some sibling quarrels.

We assume that none of your children become physically aggressive during these arguments, since you did not mention that physical aggression occurs. This is a big plus. As long as no one is getting injured, you, as the responsible parent, need to leave the boys to their own resources to resolve their conflicts. Believe it or not, sibling conflict can actually be beneficial for the children. Allow us to explain.

Sibling quarrels can serve as a "training ground", so to speak, for children. They can learn how to stand on their own two feet without the help of a parent. Children can also learn how to verbally defend a specific position, and, indirectly, they can come to realize that there can be more than one resolution to an issue. The types of quarrels that you speak of can also give children practice in assertiveness as well as gaining some insight into the value of cooperation when dealing with others.

In addition to the above, as children are playing and having disagreements, they are also learning how to follow rules, how to alternate between leader and follower, and, they are learning the importance of sharing with one another.

So, as you can see, if children *verbally* argue from time to time while they are playing, without aggression and/or injury entering the picture, they can reap untold benefits that can help prepare them for the years ahead.

Dear Doctor: When we experience very bad weather, our children are forced to stay in the house when they do not have school. This poses a problem because I can't seem to keep my children occupied so they won't feel so "cooped-up". What can I do to keep them occupied? By the way, I should tell you that my four children range in age from seven to thirteen.

Dear Bad Weather Mom: First of all, it IS NOT totally up to you to keep your children occupied. That's THEIR job. Your job is to prepare your children to work out for themselves what they will be doing on those days when they are confined indoors.

This is not to say, however, that you can't or shouldn't play games with them, or read with them, or engage in some other activity with them for part of the day. You can also set some limited time aside (about 20 to 30 minutes) to be with each child, individually, to let that child do whatever he or she would like to do, within reason, of course.

This is a time when each child, as an individual, has you all to himself or herself, without the inclusion of the other siblings. In fact, it is a good idea to make this practice a regular part of your day and not just a part of those days when the children can't go outdoors to play.

Now, let's get back to preparing for those inevitable bad-weather days that you are asking about.

One thing you can do is to set up small, special areas in your home, where each child can work on his or her own hobby or unique interest. These areas can be located in the den, in the family room, in the basement, or in the child's own room. For example, if a child enjoys drawing, the area can be set up to mimic an artist's studio. If the child has a flair for writing, the area can be arranged into a mini office. A child who enjoys working with his or her hands may have fun using an age-appropriate workbench in his or her own little workshop. We think you get the idea.

Another option is to have craft materials on hand, and, if one or more of the children are so inclined, they could work on a craft project, either alone or with another sibling, perhaps as a birthday gift for you, your spouse, or for a grandparent. If you do have a child who is creative, you can provide that child with a blank book in which that child could write poems or draw pictures. Also, in today's society with so many children being computer literate, some time can be set aside for each child to take his or her turn at the computer to play games, make cards, make banners, or email friends.

One note of caution. Always closely monitor whatever it is that your children are doing on the computer. It is a necessity in today's world.

As you can readily see, there are many things that children can do to occupy themselves when necessary. As we have said previously, your role is mainly in the preparation. Once you review what we have written, we are sure that you and your children will be able to come up with other interesting activities to pass the time on those "boring" stay-at-home days.

> Dear Doctor: It is hard to believe that the holidays are here again. And, each year I find myself in a dilemma with regards to my children. I have three sons, ages nine, six, and five, and one eleven year old daughter. Each year, without exception, I get presented with a long list of what each child wants. I then set out to buy as many of the requested items as I can find. If I don't get something, it is usually because a store has run out of stock. And, needless to say, I feel awful when I can't find something on their lists.
>
> Frankly, this practice is becoming cost prohibitive, but I would hate to see their disappointed faces when it comes to Christmas morning. I am also concerned because I feel that my children are not grasping the true meaning of the Christmas holidays. But, what alternative do I have?

Dear Mrs. Tired and Broke: We commend you for trying to satisfy your children's requests. However, there HAS TO BE some sort of limit. There is no law that we know of that dictates that parents must run amok trying to acquire everything on each child's wish-list, especially with lists growing longer and more expensive with every passing year.

Judging from your letter, it appears imperative that you need to set some financial limits---and, the sooner the better! A relatively simple solution would be to decide on a reasonable amount of money to spend on each child. Notice that we said a REASONABLE amount, not some exorbitant amount of money that you can ill afford. Under no circumstances should you be piling up Christmas gift bills that you will be paying off well into the following year, or years. You should spend only what you can comfortably afford to spend, and not a penny more.

You can talk to each of your children, on an individual basis, to determine which items are really important to them. Usually, lists can be significantly narrowed down in this manner. Then, compare the costs of these items with your REALISTIC budget, and go from there. In general, it is good practice to try to buy the top one or two items on your children's lists and then supplement these items with smaller, less expensive things that you know the children will enjoy, again making sure that everything fits within your budget.

Given your statement about the true meaning of Christmas, we will assume that you are concerned about the excessive commercialization of the holiday and its impact on your children's beliefs and attitudes. In our personal/professional (take your pick!) opinions, this is a very commendable stance to take. If you want to instill in your children a sense of what Christmas really represents, there are a number of things that you can do.

You can find out if any church, club, or organization in your area is collecting gifts for less fortunate children and families. Then, actively involve your children in the selection, wrapping, and delivering of the purchased gifts to that specific church, club, or organization for distribution to less advantaged families. In a related vein, you and your children can get together and make some gifts to donate rather than buying them.

Another option (although we hope you won't ignore the previous paragraph) would be to get some age-appropriate books about the meaning of Christmas and read them with your children and discuss the stories. In addition, there are usually some very good holiday programs on network, cable and/or public television that you can watch with your children and discuss afterwards. Whatever you choose to do, try to relax and enjoy the Christmas season with your family!

Dear Doctor: I never thought I would be asking psychologists for help, but, if I don't get some answers soon, I'm afraid my husband and I will stop speaking to each other! Our major point of disagreement concerns our seven year old identical twin daughters, "Andrea" and "Elizabeth". The girls are in the second grade and they are doing quite well in school. They do not pose behavior problems and they seem to get along well within the family as well as with their peers.

So, what's the problem? Well, I will tell you. Since the girls were born, I have been dressing them alike, fixing their hair in the same style, buying them the same kinds of toys, arranging for them to have the same playmates, and so on. I think the whole idea of them being identical in every sense is cute and I want it to last as long as possible.

However, this practice of mine has caused a gigantic, seemingly insurmountable problem between my husband and myself because he thinks that I am making a big mistake treating the girls identically. To ease the tension, I have agreed to ask an expert about our situation. So, what's your professional opinion? Should I continue as in the past, or, should I begin to separate the girls?

Dear Mother of Identical Twins: While it is cute, to a certain extent, to dress identical twins in the same outfits and, in essence, treat them as if they were one person, it is generally not the ideal thing to do. Children need their individuality and they must develop their sense of self-concept and their sense of identity as separate people, not as "one of a pair". And, this begins with appearance.

One identical twin should not feel as though he or she is looking in a mirror whenever he or she sees the other twin. While they can have some toys that are the same, it would be beneficial for each of the twins to also have some toys that the other twin does not have. For example, one may have a certain type of doll while the other may have an age-appropriate board game. This would have the added benefit of helping to encourage sharing and cooperative play.

In addition, it would also be important for you, as the parent, to ask your children about any special interests that they may have, such as sports, art, gymnastics, or music. Chances are, each of your daughters will have their own unique interests which you can explore and help cultivate. Again, by allowing the girls to pursue their own interests, the result would be a greater sense of individuality.

A good rule of thumb would be for you to let your daughters take the lead, within reason, of course, in creating their own uniqueness, rather than imposing your own parental view on them as to how identical twins should look and act.

Sorry mother, but, on this one, we tend to agree with your husband. Let each girl be her own unique person.

Dear Doctor: My son is three years old. His behavior is terrific and he seems to be a loving and happy child. However, my wife and I think that he may be having some difficulty with his language. Here's the situation.

Even though our son is only three, he sounds very immature when he speaks. He does not use sentences yet and, at best, he says only one or two words at a time. He also does a lot of pointing when he wants to ask for something, such as a drink of water. In addition, many of the words that he does say are not as clear as we think they should be.

Other family members have commented on this lack of clarity in our son's speech. Do you think there is a problem that we should be investigating? My wife and I are prepared to do whatever is necessary to take care of this situation.

Dear Concerned Father: You and your wife are wise to question your son's language development. Based on what you have noted, it does appear that your son may be experiencing some type of speech and/or language difficulty. Only a formal speech and language evaluation will give you the answers that you seek. However, with that, let us explain why we believe an evaluation should be performed.

The average three year old child should be putting at least four words together to make sentences. Speaking only one or two words at this age is below where we would expect the child to be functioning. In addition, the average three to four year old child generally has a usable vocabulary of approximately 900 words. You did not say how many words you think your son can say at this time, but, we would guess that that number is well below what the average child of his age would have at his or her disposal.

Another factor to be considered is that your son sounds immature when he speaks. A child who has some type of speech/language delay does tend to sound much younger than his or her chronological age, and, more often than not, the child's words are not understandable, particularly to the casual observer. Finally, your child's pointing to express his needs is another common behavior seen in children who are having some difficulty with their language skills.

For all of these reasons, we would tend to agree with you and your wife that the level of your son's speech/language skills warrants investigation. You should immediately contact the special education office at your local school district, explain what you see as the problem, and ask for a thorough speech and language evaluation. If the district in your area cannot help you directly, someone at the district should be able to refer you to a person and/or agency that can.

If the results of this evaluation indicate that a true problem does exist, then the professionals involved, along with you and your wife, can decide on an appropriate intervention for your son.

Do not hesitate as time is of the essence. Your son is of an age where language development should be rapidly taking place.

Dear Doctor: My eight year old son, "Chris", is very, very active. In fact, I would say that he is extremely overactive. His teacher has complained that he can't seem to stay in his seat for any length of time and that he is disturbing the other children in the class.

At home, I've noticed that he doesn't finish anything that he starts and that his attention to anything seems very short. His grades are not good but his teacher feels, as I do, that he is capable of doing much better work. It has been suggested to my husband and I that Chris may be hyperactive. How can we find out for sure? And, if he is found to be hyperactive, what can be done to cure it?

Dear Mother of Chris: To begin with, Attention Deficit/Hyperactivity Disorder, or AD/HD, is a life-span problem. It is neurologically based, and, as such, no one can get inside a child's head to "rewire the circuits". Consequently, there is no cure, per se, for true AD/HD. However, there are treatments and educational strategies available that would help a child or adolescent effectively deal with this disorder.

Some of the symptoms of AD/HD would include a poor attention span; poor impulse control; distractibility; excessive fidgeting; not completing tasks; difficulty following directions; and, poor concentration. There are additional symptoms, but, we think you get the idea.

As far as your eight year old son is concerned, the symptoms that you have described do tend to lend support to a diagnosis of AD/HD. However, the ONLY way to ascertain if your son does, in fact, have this disorder, is to have him evaluated by a competent, licensed psychologist and/or child-adolescent psychiatrist. Once evaluated, if it is determined that Chris does have AD/HD, then the professionals involved can discuss with you various treatment and educational options that would help minimize the effects of this disorder for your son, and, indirectly, for you also.

We urge you to arrange for this evaluation immediately, not only for your son's sake, but for your sake as well. You can contact the psychologist at your son's school, or you can speak with his teacher about making a referral for a psychological evaluation. Your pediatrician may also be a source for a referral to an appropriate professional.

Dear Doctor: My wife and I are becoming quite concerned about our 14 year old son, "Tommy". The problem is that we think he is considering joining what we would call a gang. He calls it "a bunch of buddies", but, to us, it seems to be a gang of some sort. The "buddies" that he refers to are a little older than Tommy and their reputations in the neighborhood and in school are not good. We certainly do not want our son involved with these kids but we feel helpless at this point.

As the parents, what should we be looking for? We don't want to further alienate our son but, at the same time, we do not want him to make a very big mistake. Do you think he is too young for gang activities? Do you think we are overreacting? If not, what can we do before it's too late?

Dear Tommy's Dad: In a word---No. He is not too young to become affiliated with a gang, and, no, we do not think you are overreacting. While most gang members are in their teens or early twenties, you can find members in the pre-teen age group as well.

For your general information, young people join gangs for a variety of reasons. Peer pressure is one important and powerful component. Also, some youngsters who feel quite insecure and/or bored with their lives may seek out a gang that he or she mistakenly believes will provide some sense of security, belongingness, and excitement. Sometimes, young people feel they need "protection" from another gang, so they, too, will join forces with others in a competing gang.

There are also children who may have an unhappy home life or they may have been exposed to a pattern of violence in the home, the neighborhood, or in the school. The net result? They may join a gang.

As the parents, you asked what you should look for. First of all, be acutely aware of any sudden changes in the friends your son has. Also, staying out very late without any viable explanation, may be a clue. In addition, a significant drop in school grades, and, perhaps, complaints from teachers regarding negative changes in his behavior may also be clues to look for. Truancy, drug and/or alcohol use/abuse, certain types of tattoos, a change in the manner of speaking, and, carrying weapons would also signal trouble.

But, keep in mind that these are just indicators---not definitive proof of gang membership and/or activity. Some of the above can also be signs of other types of problems, including, but not limited to, depression and other emotional problems.

Being the parents, there are some things that you and your wife can do as preventive measures. First of all, keep the lines of communication open at all times and be very supportive of your son. Whenever and wherever possible, build your child's self-esteem and confidence by positively reinforcing his efforts and accomplishments. Being good role models for your son would be immensely important as he is growing and maturing.

Above all, show and express your love and affection for your son. A child will be much less likely to gravitate toward a gang if he or she perceives that he or she is receiving love, support, and encouragement at home. As the parents, you need to provide a home environment within which Tommy can feel and believe that he is an important part of your family.

If you and your wife believe that Tommy is considering joining a gang, talk honestly with him without being judgmental or accusatory. You can also look for age-appropriate activities and groups in your area that your son may be interested in joining. You can also confidentially enlist the help of his teachers, your clergyperson (priest, minister, rabbi, etc.), or any other respectable and responsible adult that is admired by your son and trusted by you. Together, you may be able to effectively intervene before your son takes that dreadfully wrong step. Good luck.

EPILOGUE

Well, there you have it. We have come to the end of the journey---at least as far as this book is concerned. In reality, however, you never really come to the end of your journey toward being as good a parent as you can be, in every sense of the phrase.

Once you have a child, you, as a loving and caring individual, will realize that you have embarked on a life-long journey. As we are sure you know, sometimes that journey will be fairly easy. But, as you also probably know, much of the time, it will be filled with varying degrees of difficulty, for whatever reason.

But, when all is said and done, we think that you will agree with us that it is definitely a journey well worth taking.

Appendix I

SHORT-TERM MEMORY LIMITS FOR CHILDREN

Age	Number of Items
3	2
4	3
5	3 to 4
6	3 to 4
7	5

*Note: These are close approximations for the average child at the above age levels.

ACTIVITY – TIME CHART

Time	Activity	Stress Level
		1 2 3 4 5
7:00 am		
7:30 am		
8:00 am		
8:30 am		
9:00 am		
9:30 am		
10:00 am		
10:30 am		
11:00 am		
11:30 am		
12:00 pm		

12:30 pm

1:00 pm

1:30 pm

2:00 pm

2:30 pm

3:00 pm

3:30 pm

4:00 pm

4:30 pm

5:00 pm

5:30 pm

6:00 pm

6:30 pm

7:00 pm

7:30 pm

8:00 pm

8:30 pm

9:00 pm

9:30 pm

10:00 pm

10:30 pm

11:00 pm

PROBLEM CHECK LIST

Problem	Possible Alternatives	Use	Did It Work? Yes No

EXAMPLES OF POSSIBLE ALTERNATIVES

1. Ignore the situation.
2. Withdraw from the situation/issue.
3. Say "No!"
4. Be assertive, not aggressive.
5. Apologize, if appropriate.
6. Pay the bill.
7. Laugh.
8. Listen to the other side of the story.
9. Buy the present.
10. Compromise.
11. Do not see the particular person in question.
12. Try to make amends with the person in question.
13. Put the problem on the "back burner" for a while.
14. Decide if you really do have control over the situation.
15. Take control, if appropriate.
16. Get up earlier in the morning.
17. Go to bed earlier at night.

WHICH ONE?

O K, folks. Way back in Chapter 3, we told you that one of us did not like the word "space". Remember?

And, in Chapter 5, we told you that one of us tends to think of something additional that is relevant to a topic, but, after the fact---not during it! Remember?

Well, now that we are at the end of the book, we have decided that we WOULD NOT tell you which one of us we were talking about! However, we are quite sure that the people who know us well have already come to the correct conclusion.

Happy Parenting Folks!!

INDEX